At Issue

Campaign Finance

Other Books in the At Issue Series:

At Issue

| Campaign Finance

David Haugen and Susan Musser, Book Editors

GREENHAVEN PRESS
A part of Gale, Cengage Learning

GALE
CENGAGE Learning

Detroit • New York • San Francisco • New Haven, Conn • Waterville, Maine • London

Christine Nasso, *Publisher*
Elizabeth Des Chenes, *Managing Editor*

For more information, contact:
Greenhaven Press
27500 Drake Rd.
Farmington Hills, MI 48331-3535
Or you can visit our Internet site at gale.cengage.com

For product information and technology assistance, contact us at

Gale Customer Support, 1-800-877-4253
For permission to use material from this text or product, submit all requests online at www.cengage.com/permissions

Further permissions questions can be e-mailed to permissionrequest@cengage.com

Articles in Greenhaven Press anthologies are often edited for length to meet page requirements. In addition, original titles of these works are changed to clearly present the main thesis and to explicitly indicate the author's opinion. Every effort is made to ensure that Greenhaven Press accurately reflects the original intent of the authors. Every effort has been made to trace the owners of copyrighted material.

Cover Image copyright Illustration Works.

LIBRARY OF CONGRESS CATALOGING-IN-PUBLICATION DATA

Campaign finance / David Haugen and Susan Musser, book editors.
    p. cm. -- (At issue)
  Includes bibliographical references and index.
  ISBN 978-0-7377-4872-7 (hardcover) -- ISBN 978-0-7377-4873-4 (pbk.)
  1. Campaign funds--United States. I. Haugen, David M., 1969- II. Musser, Susan.
  JK1991.C3425 2010
  324.7'80973--dc22

                                                   2010006726

Contents

Introduction

Money has influenced the outcomes of political elections from the inception of the United States. George Washington reportedly handed out rum to Virginians to win their votes when he ran for the state's House of Burgesses in 1758. Abraham Lincoln ran for the U.S. Senate on donations from wealthy patrons. Even the trust-busting Theodore Roosevelt financed his 1904 bid for presidential reelection mainly on money obtained from bankers and industrialists—a source his predecessor William McKinley had tapped several years earlier.

It was during Roosevelt's administration that journalists and reformers began loudly voicing objections to the influence of money on public elections. Roosevelt—a progressive securely in office by then—quickly tried to distance himself from the source of his campaign funding. Newspapers, however, uncovered the truth. Caught in a scandal and not wanting to appear indebted to big business, the president spoke out against the culling of campaign donations from the kind of financiers that helped put him in office. A year after his reelection, he told Congress, "All contributions by corporations to any political committee or for any political purpose should be forbidden by law; directors should not be permitted to use stockholders' money for such purposes." With presidential support, Senator Benjamin R. Tillman, a Democrat from South Carolina, pushed a bill through Congress in 1907 that barred banks and corporations from making any "contribution or expenditure" relating to a federal election. The Tillman Act became the first national legislative effort to reform the manner in which political campaigns were funded.

Since 1907, the issue of campaign finance reform has repeatedly passed through the halls of Congress. A handful of laws in the early and mid-twentieth century tried to place caps on campaign contributions and limit the types of organizations that could make legal donations to candidates for federal office. Most of these acts lacked enforcement measures and were easily circumvented. In 1971, Congress passed the sweeping Federal Election Campaign Act (FECA) to correct the shortcomings of previous legislation. The FECA called for public disclosure of campaign funding sources and set limits on contributions—even the amount of a candidate's own money that could be used to run a political race. The law also established the Federal Election Commission (FEC) to police the spending of both parties.

The FECA was not a universally popular law. In 1976, the U.S. Supreme Court heard the case of *Buckley v. Valeo*, in which plaintiffs, headed by Senator James L. Buckley, charged that the FECA was in violation of First and Fifth Amendment rights. These officials believed capping campaign contributions and requiring disclosure impinged on free speech and individual liberty. In its landmark decision, the Court upheld contribution limits and disclosure clauses but found that barring candidates from spending their own funds to finance their campaigns was unconstitutional, as was placing any kind of limit on how much a candidate could amass to run a race. The Court also stated that contribution limits could not be set so low as to restrict the ability of candidates to spread their message to the public. In response, the FEC raised the cap of individual contributions—so called "hard-money" donations—to $1,000 in 1979. The commission also decided to allow unlimited contributions in the name of party building, however. Such activities—termed "soft-money" contributions—might include financing voter registration drives or paying for media advertisements to promote issues.

Soft-money contributions grew tremendously over the next two decades, as both parties spent huge sums on radio and television advertising that often savaged rival candidates without using the forbidden terms of "vote for" or "vote against" outlined by the Supreme Court and the FEC. Supposed issue ads became "attack ads," and critics again feared that money was unfairly winning elections because candidates with the most soft money could easily swamp the messages of their opponents. Concerned over the growth of soft-money spending, Senator John McCain of Arizona and Senator Russ Feingold of Wisconsin spearheaded legislation in 2002 to redress what they saw as a failing election finance system. Feingold told the Senate assembly in 2001, "We can take a major step toward closing the loopholes that have really made a mockery of our campaign finance reform laws. We have the power to close these loopholes and we have the duty to close them." The resulting Bipartisan Campaign Reform Act (BCRA—also known as the McCain-Feingold Act) passed through Congress and was signed into law by President George W. Bush.

The BCRA increased hard-money contribution limits to $2,000 per individual but prohibited national parties and their subsidiary organizations from accepting soft money—that is, money not subject to the limits imposed by the FEC. Even traditional party-building activities—such as voter registration—now had to be financed by federal funds given to each candidate to manage and run a campaign. In addition, money gathered from corporations or labor unions could not be used to fund advertisements referencing a specific candidate by name or likeness. These ads could be funded by independent organizations, but they had to disclose the source of the funds if the amount exceeded prescribed limits. Supporters of the BCRA, such as Norman Ornstein, a resident scholar at the Brookings Institution, maintain that the new restrictions have had a positive effect on fundraising. He claims that because they lack soft-money support, the political parties have had to take on the job of soliciting funds from voters, ensuring that the political machines engage with the public that ostensibly puts candidates in office. He also contends that the campaign ad regulations have not stopped political messages from getting through. "Ad spots by independent groups still fill the air-waves. The new rules do not bar a single ad or message: They simply apply to outside groups and parties the same standards that apply to candidates and political action committees when it comes to a narrow group of electioneering broadcast ads," Ornstein asserts.

Critics of the McCain-Feingold Act believe that its reform measures are a threat to free speech. Andrew Lewis, a member of the Ayn Rand Institute and a supporter of free capitalism, states that "Political contributions, large or small, are a mode of speech . . . because they explicitly entail the expression of ideas." Lewis finds it unlawful to restrict this type of political advocacy. He stresses, "Your contribution to a candidate is de facto the publication of your ideas and is similar to hiring a speaker or commissioning an author. The amount of money you contribute—as an individual or in cooperation with oth-ers—should not disqualify you from expressing your ideas. The only proper 'limits' on contributions are those set by your willingness to employ your money for this purpose." Similarly, Lewis and others in his camp fear that any regulation of broadcast advertisement curtails the right of individuals and organizations to express their ideas in the public sphere.

Since the passage of the Bipartisan Campaign Reform Act, the Supreme Court has heard several cases seeking to overturn parts of the law. The Court has upheld most of the BCRA's provisions, but in 2007, five of the nine justices determined that the barring of corporate or union sponsorship of cam-paign ads was unconstitutional unless it could be proven that such ads were explicitly advocating the support or defeat of a candidate. Some claim that this ruling is a victory for free speech; others rue it as a victory for big-money politics. This contention continues to haunt the law as well as campaign fi-nance reform in general. As the articles in *At Issue: Campaign Finance* illustrate, the worry that money can determine demo-cratic elections has dogged even the most recent presidential race. The issues raised in this anthology reflect the current scope of the debate on campaign finance for a range of elected positions. Lawmakers and judges are likely to grapple with these arguments as they determine whether campaign finance laws have gone too far in abridging individual liberty or whether further reform is needed to ensure that ideas, not money, elect those persons who are supposed to represent the will of a democracy.

1

Campaign Finance and the Race for the 2008 Presidential Election

Costas Panagopoulos

Costas Panagopoulos is an assistant professor of political science and the director of the Center for Electoral Politics and Democracy at Fordham University in New York.

Despite the restrictions enacted by the Bipartisan Campaign Reform Act of 2002 (BCRA), both major political parties raised record amounts of money during the 2008 presidential election race. Bundling contributions, channeling money through special tax-exempt organizations, and other legal loopholes allowed millions in soft-money donations to reach Republicans and Democrats alike. The reform law—which seeks to limit individual donations—has also prompted the parties to petition small donors for needed funding, thus bringing more individuals into the election process. Regardless of the pros and cons of the BCRA, the system of public financing for presidential candidates is in need of an overhaul to guarantee that the parties use money to bring issues to light and not to buy elections.

Ralph Waldo Emerson [an American philosopher and poet] once asked, "Can anyone remember when times were not hard and money not scarce?" The answer to the latter might turn out to be the 2008 presidential election, which may prove to be the most expensive political campaign in U.S. history. After only nine months of fund-raising in 2007 (the last period for which complete figures are available at press time), candidates had raised over $420 million—more than half of the $674 million raised in the complete 2004 election cycle and more than the $352 million total raised in 2000. Before the votes are counted this November [2008], the money chase could bring in more than $1 billion.

Some contributions are purposefully aimed to advance or support a policy agenda, while other donors enjoy the social benefits associated with giving: networking, name recognition and more.

Who Got What?

To a great extent, the fund-raising dynamics of an election cycle are a function of the larger political dynamics. With wide-open contests for both parties' nominations, no incumbents at the top of the ballot, a slew of animated and high-profile candidates and an evenly divided electorate, voter enthusiasm is high on both sides of the aisle. But Democrats may have more reason to be excited. A shaky economy, record-low and declining approval ratings for the Republican President [George W.] Bush, an unpopular war in Iraq and a seemingly imminent recession may make 2008 an especially difficult year for Republicans. Political scientists have shown that dollars raised are related to prospects for victory, which helps to explain why Democrats running for president across the board have been raking in the dough and helping to dismantle the fund-raising advantage Republicans have historically enjoyed. At the end of the third quarter of 2007, Democratic presidential contenders had raised more funds than Republicans by a 1.5-to-1 margin ($244 million to $175 million respectively).

The two leading Democrats, New York Senator Hillary Clinton—the first candidate ever to announce she would eschew public funds for both the primary and general election campaigns—and Illinois Senator Barack Obama, have raised unprecedented sums. Clinton had collected nearly $91 million at the end of the third quarter, [whereas] Obama brought in over $80 million. The other Democrats also raised impressive amounts. Despite the uphill battle Republicans may be facing in 2008, Republican contenders also attracted considerable sums from donors.

The B.C.R.A. was supposed to end the era of soft money, double individual contribution limits and index them to inflation. Before long, however, new loopholes were found and exploited.

Where Does the Money Come From?

Donors contribute to political campaigns for many reasons. Some contributions are purposefully aimed to advance or support a policy agenda, while other donors enjoy the social benefits associated with giving: networking, name recognition and more.

Material motives—quid pro quo [something received or given for something else] expectations to get something in return—induce at least some donors to give, but campaign finance laws are designed to prevent such impropriety. This is one reason ... the Bipartisan Campaign Reform Act of 2002 [B.C.R.A.] outlawed so-called soft money. [Although] the Watergate-era [named for 1970s political scandal] Federal Election Campaign Act placed strict limits and disclosure requirements on individual contributions (the maximum was $1,000 for the primary election and $1,000 for the general), a loophole in the law allowed the political parties, rather than the candidates, to raise soft money in virtually unlimited amounts for certain "party-building" activities, which frequently indirectly helped individual candidates. During several previous presidential campaigns, the amount of soft money skyrocketed. In 2000, for example, the Democratic National Committee raised $136.6 million in soft-money contributions; the Republican National Committee raised $166.2 million in soft money in the same cycle. The B.C.R.A. was supposed to end the era of soft money, double individual contribution limits and index them to inflation.

Before long, however, new loopholes were found and exploited. The 2004 election included intense spending and activities by so-called 527 organizations (named after the applicable section of the I.R.S. [Internal Revenue Service] tax code). These are groups created primarily to influence the nomination, election, appointment or defeat of candidates for public office. In the 2004 election, 527s raised and spent over $600 million. Typically, these groups spend most heavily during the general election campaign; and it is expected that barring any legislative or regulatory intervention, 527s will be active again in 2008.

Increased reliance on bundlers and outsourcing fund-raising may be legal, but they are not without risk.

Bundling and Professional Fund-Raising

Besides organized interest groups, individuals are finding ways within the constraints of the law to remain valuable to their candidates of choice. One of the more contentious issues surrounding the 2008 fund-raising cycle is the practice called bundling. *The Wall Street Journal* reported in 2007 that bundling, by which a single fund-raiser gathers up contributions for a candidate from employees, clients and acquaintances, has become the latest way for campaigns to raise big money. Ample evidence points to a bundling boom. Based on data through September 2007, a *Wall Street Journal* analysis concludes that there are nearly twice as many bundlers in the current election [2008] as there were in the 2004 cycle, a nearly tenfold increase since 2000. Bundled donations in 2007 accounted for 28.3 percent of total candidate intake, compared with 18.2 percent in 2004 and 7.7 percent in 2000. Nearly every major 2008 candidate has a bundling program.

Candidates are also relying much more on professional fund-raisers to fill their campaign coffers. An analysis by the Center for Responsive Politics reveals considerable growth in the outsourcing of campaign fund-raising. Campaign organizations hired about 800 fund-raising consultants to bring in $31 million in the first three quarters of 2007, up from about 260 such firms (and $12.3 million) for the same period in 2003. Republicans have out-outsourced Democrats by a wide margin, with Mitt Romney, the biggest outsourcer, tapping fund-raising consultants to bring in $3.1 million in the first three quarters of 2007. By contrast, Barack Obama and Hillary Clinton have outsourced $600,000 and $500,000 respectively in the same period.

The B.C.R.A. did not address the system of public financing for presidential campaigns that has been in place since 1976—a system that is essentially defunct and may even be on the verge of collapse.

Increased reliance on bundlers and outsourcing fund-raising may be legal, but they are not without risk, because donors are further removed from the campaigns and may not be properly vetted. Hillary Clinton, for example, was forced to return over $850,000 in cash to Norman Hsu, one of her major bundlers, when it became known that Hsu, a New York apparel giant, may have been involved in an illegal investment scheme.

On the plus side, B.C.R.A. changes as well as technological developments seem to be bringing more small donors (those who give less than $200) into the fray. The Campaign Finance Institute estimates that 21 percent of all contributions through the third quarter in 2007 came from small donors—many of them making their contributions online—up from 18 percent over the corresponding period in 2003. Small donors accounted for one-quarter or more of total intake (through the third quarter of 2007) for Obama, [John] Edwards, [Fred] Thompson, [Ron] Paul, [Mike] Huckabee, [Tom] Tancredo, [Dennis] Kucinich, [Duncan] Hunter and [Mike] Gravel. Over the complete period of the 2004 cycle, 31 percent of total [George W.] Bush contributions came from small donors, 32 percent of [John] Kerry's contributions and 61 percent of [Howard] Dean's.

Has the System Changed?

Though the number of small donors has risen, presidential candidates continue to draw the lion's share (two thirds) of their individual contributions from donors of large amounts (over $1,000). And for the most part, campaign organizations appear to be finding ways to overcome the soft-money ban. B.C.R.A. has actually done little to improve the system of presidential campaign finance.

The B.C.R.A. did not address the system of public financing for presidential campaigns that has been in place since 1976—a system that is essentially defunct and may even be on the verge of collapse. Federal law enables eligible presidential candidates to accept public funding for their campaigns provided they adhere to strict state-by-state spending limits. Given the inordinate importance of low-population, early-contest states like Iowa and New Hampshire, candidates are reluctant to restrict their spending in these states, especially if their opponents are not doing so. In the 2000 election, George W. Bush announced he would forgo public funding in order to be exempted from state spending caps. By 2004, three main candidates—Bush, Kerry and Dean—rejected public financing for the same reasons, and in this election most candidates have also rejected public funds. In a historic and unprecedented announcement, Hillary Clinton declared she would even reject public financing in the general election campaign in order to be free of spending constraints.

Michael Malbin, director of the nonpartisan Campaign Finance Institute, has argued forcefully that this system is obsolete and is desperately in need of reform. An institute task force has proposed a number of reforms to preserve the public financing system, including raising the spending limit in nomination cycles, creating an "escape hatch" for public financing candidates who run against opponents who reject public money, changing the matching fund formula and raising the voluntary income tax checkoff to finance some of these changes. In its current form, the public financing system, originally intended to level the playing field in presidential elections, is not achieving this purpose. This fuels fears that the nominations, and even the election, will go to the highest bidder.

The Good News

Yet there is always a silver lining. Regarding the impact of contributions on governing, political scientists have found little evidence of a true quid pro quo in which politicians deliver in return for donations. Elected representatives are constrained by vigorous ethics laws, and other factors ([such as] constituency preferences, partisanship and ideology) are likely to be far more influential in a leader's decision-making calculations. Money may buy access to a politician, but it rarely guarantees outcomes.

There are also limits on how much success money can buy a candidate on the campaign trail. Consider the victory of Huckabee in Iowa despite the fact that his campaign was run on a shoestring budget. Experience from the 2004 cycle also suggests caution. Dean failed to capture the nomination despite being the year-end money leader.

As the eminent political scientist V.O. Key noted decades ago, voters are not fools. They realize that money is necessary to sustain a national dialogue about ideas and policy proposals. The one thing money buys for sure is a national conversation, a debate over candidates and policies, that is essential to the democratic process. The big bucks filling the 2008 presidential campaign coffers show that at least we have that.

2

The Bipartisan Campaign Reform Act Is a Success

Meredith McGehee

Meredith McGehee is the policy director for the Campaign Legal Center, a nonpartisan organization that analyzes issues relating to campaign finance and the electoral process.

The Bipartisan Campaign Reform Act of 2002 is achieving the goals it set out to accomplish. It has restricted the amount of "soft-money" contributions—those large donations from wealthy individuals and corporations that often gave certain candidates an unfair advantage in campaign spending—and has forced office seekers to engage Americans citizens in an effort to win financial support from legions of small donors. This shift ensures that election campaigns will reflect the will of the people and not the interests of big money.

It's been seven years since the McCain-Feingold bill was passed [in 2002], yet the measure (known as the Bipartisan Campaign Reform Act or BCRA) is still the subject of a massive amount of disinformation.

Every time there is a report on the problems with the current campaign finance system, political pundits line up to find a way to blame it on McCain-Feingold. And their critiques of the law constantly morph. There are still millions of dollars in

Meredith McGehee, "Washington's Best Kept Secret: McCain-Feingold Works," The Campaign Legal Center Blog, April 28, 2009. Reproduced by permission.

politics? Blame BCRA. Bundling[1] is flourishing? Blame BCRA. 527 organizations[2] continue to [break] the law? Blame BCRA. The Federal Election Commission remains feckless? Blame BCRA.

Admittedly, BCRA's critics have been remarkably successful at influencing the public perception of the bill enacted in 2002 that banned unlimited "soft-money" contributions by corporations, unions and wealthy individuals. They repeatedly label BCRA a failure by redefining and misrepresenting what BCRA was supposed to do. They couldn't be more wrong. In fact, the opposite is true—BCRA has been remarkably successful.

While unlimited soft-money contributions and thus large donors were the primary source of party money in 2002, small contributions from individuals were the principal source of funds in the 2006 races.

Enhancing Civic Participation in Elections

For example, critics like Senate Minority Leader Mitch McConnell (R-Ky.) testified that passage of the law would mean the death of the national party committees. Yet in the last two elections since BCRA was enacted, the national parties have flourished, raising more hard money than they raised previously in hard and soft money combined.

The parties, weaned [from] the corporate and union treasury funds, were forced to engage with actual people. In the process, they have begun to rediscover what political parties

1. Bundling is the practice of combining several campaign donations from a group of related organizations into one large donation. The individual donations do not violate the legal limits placed on contributions from a single source, but the combined influence of those related groups is enhanced by the total "bundled" donation.
2. Named after a section of the U.S. tax code, 527 organizations are political groups that avoid regulation by the Federal Election Commission and thus are not restricted in the size of their campaign contributions because they supposedly do not support candidates directly but merely endorse specific issues or mobilize voter turnout at the polls. Critics often charge that 527 organizations do not maintain the proper separation from candidate advocacy demanded by the tax law.

21

are supposed to be about—groups of like-minded individuals working to get their candidates elected. That is called citizen participation—a healthy activity in a democracy. And in the non-presidential year of 2006, the parties did just fine, thank you—raking in more than $900 million. While unlimited soft money contributions and thus large donors were the primary source of party money in 2002, small contributions from individuals were the principal source of funds in the 2006 races. In sum, the parties became more robust and raised even more money for their political activities than in the pre-BCRA days.

Even more telling was the historic campaign of President Barack Obama. His fundraising efforts, achieved by going after more small donors than ever before, were totally consistent with what BCRA envisioned: more people than ever participating in the system.

Despite the never-ending chorus from its critics, McCain-Feingold was never an attempt to remove money from politics. The goal was to break the dependence of elected officials on massive contributions from corporations, unions and wealthy individuals, and thereby reduce the potential for corruption in the democratic process. Clearly the law has succeeded on this front.

A First Step Toward Greater Reform

BCRA was a triage bill—a bill designed to deal with the most egregious problems in the system at that moment in time. The original version, which had a comprehensive solution with spending limits and public resources for candidates, had no chance of passing in the early years of this decade [2002–2004] with House Majority Leader Tom DeLay's "K Street Project"[3] in full swing. But the need to address the out-

---

3. In 1995 Tom DeLay (R-Texas) informed Washington lobbying groups that—because Republicans controlled congress—their access to high-ranking politicians would depend on agreeing to hire more Republicans to represent their interests, thus giving Republicans more voice in these lobbying groups and ultimately influencing how they spent their funds during election years.

of-control soft money and the campaign ads masquerading as "issue discussion" was urgent.

While setting the record straight won't stop the disinformation campaign on BCRA, it should remind [all] who continue to care about the role that large money plays in [U.S.] elections that change—meaningful change—can indeed be achieved, even if it is not as big and bold as many people wish. Reform comes slowly in this town [Washington, D.C.], at least when it comes to Congress reforming itself. But there's a big difference this time around: the man in the White House says he wants to lead the reform race. And that gives real hope to those of us interested in building on successful reforms like BCRA.

3

The Bipartisan Campaign Reform Act Is a Necessary but Incomplete Law

Trevor Potter

A former chairman of the Federal Election Commission, Trevor Potter is currently the president of the Campaign Legal Center, a nonpartisan organization that analyzes issues relating to campaign finance and the electoral process. He is the author of such books as The New Campaign Finance Sourcebook *and* Federal Election Law and the Internet.

The Bipartisan Campaign Reform Act of 2002 was an imperfect attempt to stem the flow of big money in influencing the outcome of public elections. Indeed, the act stymied some large contributors and other "soft-money" sources that otherwise would have brazenly filled the candidates' coffers of their choice. In that respect, the law forced politicians to seek broader public support. Wealthy donors and well-funded lobbying groups have found ways to circumvent the law, however, and some politicians have done their best to limit its power. These abuses, coupled with vague details within the law itself, reveal the flaws of the legislation, indicating that further reform is necessary to revamp the campaign finance system.

When the McCain-Feingold campaign finance legislation was being debated four years ago [in 2002], Senator Mitch McConnell (R-Ky.) told his colleagues that it would "eviscerate the national party committees" because of its ban on unlimited "soft-money" donations.

The legislation passed, and in 2004, the parties raised more funds than ever before. In response, critics explained that it was a presidential election year, and an exceptionally motivating one at that; funds would surely dry up in 2006. Yet numbers recently released by the Federal Election Commission (FEC) show that the $555.2 million raised by both parties so far this cycle [as of mid-2006] is ahead of 2004 totals by 5 percent.

The law has been an undisputed success in combating the corruption of huge soft-money contributions and an apparent success in re-energizing grass-roots supporters.

Still, skeptics say: The legislation was supposed to put an end to corrupt money in politics, yet here we have a series of scandals unfolding on Capitol Hill like implausible B-movie scripts.

Shutting Out Big Money Contributors

In response, I'd point out that McCain-Feingold—or the Bipartisan Campaign Reform Act (BCRA), as the law is formally known—didn't seek to remove money from politics. After all, we have no public funding for House and Senate candidates, and the presidential funding system is broken. Candidates and parties still need money to reach voters. The limited goal of the legislation was to remove the obvious corruption of six-figure individual contributions, and corporate and labor donations (increasingly solicited by elected federal officials) to national committee coffers. Sponsors argued that focusing on small individual contributions would force the parties back to the grass roots and away from White House soft-money "coffees [personal meetings between the president and big-money donors]."

And the law has been an undisputed success in combating the corruption of huge soft-money contributions and an apparent success in re-energizing grass-roots supporters. Individuals are now limited in what they can give party committees: $26,700 to a committee per year—no small sum for most Americans, but still far short of the hundreds of thousands and occasional millions wealthy individuals contributed to party committees in pre-BCRA years. Corporate and union contributions to national committees are banned [in 2010 the Supreme Court ruled such restrictions to be unconstitutional]. Not only are these individuals and entities not buying influence with their huge contributions, congressional and executive branch officials are not soliciting such contributions from regulated entities at the same time that legislation or contracts of direct interest to those entities are before a Cabinet officer or committee chair.

The BCRA was never expected to solve every problem.

Courting Public Support

As for reinvigoration of the grass roots: There is every evidence that both parties in 2004 sought (and got) greater individual involvement from volunteers and contributors than in previous years. The media have extensively covered the new emphasis on the "ground game" in key states. Both parties report millions of new donors—many acting through the Internet. Some argue that this [change] isn't the doing of the BCRA, [as] party committees would have increased their Internet activities with or without the new law. Perhaps. But incentives usually matter, and if it is comparatively easy to raise money one way (by telephoning a handful of soft-money donors) and more difficult to do it another (by investing money to build a better Internet fundraising structure), the easy way usually wins out.

But why do we still have [fraud and bribery scandal] cases such as those of Jack Abramoff and Randy Cunningham, and serious allegations being made in the media against Representatives William Jefferson (D-La.) and Bob Ney (R-Ohio)?

BCRA Is Only a Start

Unfortunately, in four short years, people have forgotten just how bad the soft-money system was. Nowadays we are usually talking about small contributions ($5,000 by a PAC [political action committee], or $2,100 by an individual)—not six- and seven-figure numbers. Go back and read the court record in Sen. McConnell's failed Supreme Court challenge to the BCRA to see how much larger and more blatant some of the corruption was.

The BCRA was never expected to solve every problem. Its sponsors explicitly said that there was no silver bullet [a sure and swift fix], that the law was only a start—necessarily limited to the worst abuses in the system. The Supreme Court majority in the McConnell challenge also recognized this when it noted, "Money, like water, will always find an outlet."

In any system of government, there will be instances of bribery, even when it is clearly outlawed. Such acts must be vigorously investigated, prosecuted and punished. The system can also be reformed—as proposals to limit earmarks, provide greater transparency in the legislative process and establish an ethics regulation process with teeth all seek to do.

There will always be efforts to circumvent new laws, as we saw in the most recent election cycle with the creation of some "527" groups, ostensibly independent of the national political parties but closely linked to them in personnel, donors and election goals. When the BCRA was passed, there was an obvious risk that national parties and their supporters would try to re-create the soft-money system through new party-controlled entities. The congressional and litigation efforts to further regulate some 527s are aimed at preventing this outcome.

Of course the BCRA has not solved all problems. For one thing, the FEC's anti-McCain-Feingold majority has done its best to sabotage the new law, and questions about what the law requires and prohibits continue to be fought out at the commission and in the courts. Moreover, the BCRA by design left several large questions about campaign finance—such as whether the existing presidential public funding system will be reformed to make it relevant and useful to 21st-century campaigns—for other Congresses. Finally, we continue to gain new experience and information about money and politics. This ongoing experience points out areas where new structures or reforms might well be useful.

It's not a bad thing that still more changes are needed. Neither human beings nor their governmental systems will ever be static—especially in an area as dynamic as campaign financing. Perfection may not be attainable, but better laws are. McCain-Feingold was a necessary—but not sufficient—start.

4

Campaign Finance Reform Stifles Political Free Speech

Bradley A. Smith

Bradley A. Smith served as chairman of the Federal Election Commission from 2000 to 2005. He is presently a professor of law at Capital University in Columbus, Ohio.

In the name of leveling the electoral playing field, Democrats have pushed campaign finance reform measures through Congress. Such legislation has limited campaign contributions from advocacy groups and wealthy backers and fought against the proliferation of campaign advertisements close to election time. Curbing money used to promote a candidate or banning campaign ads at any time during an election is a violation of free speech, however. Democrats have mainly used this tactic to keep conservative grassroots organizations from helping unseat liberal politicians, and this bias is evident because Democrats have little interest in purging the election process of other—more significant—influences such as the liberal spin of the media. If America wants democracy, then it should tolerate free speech during elections, permitting each party to reach the voters using the resources at its command.

In February 2006, Norm Feck learned that the city of Parker, Colorado, was thinking about annexing his neighborhood, Parker North. Feck attended a meeting on the annexation, realized that it would mean more bureaucracy, and concluded that it wouldn't be in Parker North residents' interest. Together with five other Parker North locals, he wrote letters to the editor, handed out information sheets, formed an Internet discussion group, and printed up anti-annexation yard signs, which soon began sprouting throughout the neighborhood.

That's when annexation supporters took action—not with their own public campaign, but with a legal complaint against Feck and his friends for violating Colorado's campaign finance laws. The suit also threatened anyone who had contacted Feck's group about the annexation, or put up one of their yard signs, with "investigation, scrutinization, and sanctions for Campaign Finance violations." Apparently the anti-annexation activists hadn't registered with the state, or filled out the required paperwork disclosing their expenditures on time. Steep fines, increasing on a daily basis, were possible. The case remains in litigation.

Should Americans care about what's happening in Parker North? They certainly don't seem to. A LexisNexis search finds just three stories, all in Colorado papers, that mention the dispute. That's it: no commentary by columnists, no national network reports, not even coverage by a single major blogger on this application of campaign finance law to the most basic community political activity. The lack of interest is in a way understandable, since campaign finance reform, whether on the state or federal level, is at once forbiddingly complex and seemingly irrelevant to most citizens' lives. People tend to see reform as affecting only the powerful—lobbyists, big corporations, "fat cats"—not ordinary Joes. With some notable exceptions, even conservatives, who overwhelmingly believe that the First Amendment protects one's right to spend money on a candidate, don't pay much attention.

But as Norm Feck's story shows, that's a riskily blasé attitude. Campaign finance reform is creating an intrusive regulatory regime that's steadily eroding Americans' political freedoms. Making matters worse, it does little or nothing to combat corruption. Its proponents, mostly on the left, have chiefly used it to bolster their own political fortunes and to undermine limited, constitutional government.

Campaign Finance Reform Strikes at the Heart of Republican Power

This year [2007] marks the 100th anniversary of the first federal campaign finance law, the Tillman Act. Named for its sponsor, South Carolina Democratic senator Ben Tillman, the act banned corporate contributions to federal campaigns, and as such remains the backbone of federal campaign finance regulations. Tillman was a racist who advocated lynching black voters and almost single-handedly established Jim Crow [segregation laws] in the South. The new law fit neatly with his segregationist agenda, [as] corporate "money power" primarily backed anti-segregationist Republican politicians.

[The Federal Election Campaign Act (FECA) of 1971] left American politics more heavily regulated than at any time in history.

The modern era of campaign finance reform has an equally partisan origin. From the mid-1960s on, opinion polls showed steady erosion in public support for big government and liberalism. Republicans made substantial congressional gains in 1966, and two years later Richard Nixon won the presidency. By 1970, Democrats feared—with good reason—that their longstanding electoral majority was in jeopardy. There were three ways that they might turn things around, observes [libertarian think tank] Cato Institute election-law expert John Samples: persuading the public to embrace their big-government philosophy, changing that increasingly unpopular philosophy, or "preventing or at least hobbling the translation of the shifting public mood into electoral losses and policy changes."

The Democrats chose Number Three and looked to campaign finance reform as a way to achieve it. The Federal Election Campaign Act (FECA), which Congress passed in 1971 (and amended three years later), would, Democrats hoped, strike at the heart of Republican political power—while leaving untouched their own sources of influence, such as union-organized volunteers. The law tightly limited both political contributions and any expenditure that might "influence" an election. It also mandated disclosure of political contributions as small as $10, established a system in which taxes financed part of presidential races, and set up a bureaucracy, the Federal Election Commission (FEC), to enforce the new rules. In *Buckley v. Valeo* (1976), the Supreme Court struck down the expenditure limits on First Amendment grounds, and held that the disclosure requirements, as well as limits on contributions to non-candidate political organizations (the National Rifle Association [NRA], say), would apply only when the group receiving the donations "explicitly advocated" the election or defeat of a candidate, through such phrases as "vote for Smith." Still, even as truncated by the Court, the new law left American politics more heavily regulated than at any time in history.

---

*Campaign finance reform neatly accomplishes Democrats'
goal of muffling political speech on the Right.*

Congressional Democrats also drove the next major extension of campaign-finance regulations, the 2002 McCain-Feingold law—though of course one of the bill's cosponsors, Arizona senator John McCain, was a prominent, if unconventional, Republican. McCain-Feingold banned a kind of fundraising in which the GOP [Grand Old Party, i.e., Republican] had a growing advantage: "soft-money" contributions to political parties that could fund party building and political-issue ads stopping short of express advocacy. It also restricted the ability of incorporated organizations—like the NRA—to broadcast ads that so much as named a candidate within 60 days of an election, and it raised the limit on direct, "hard-money" donations to candidates. Democrats were by now a Congressional minority. But enough endangered Republicans—hating the ads that targeted *them*—joined the Dems and McCain to get the bill passed.

The extent of the regulatory web now in place is evident even when advocates of free speech score an occasional victory. In June [2007], the Supreme Court, by a narrow 5–4 margin, held in *Federal Election Commission v. Wisconsin Right to Life* that the government may not prevent citizens' organizations from broadcasting ads that discuss pending legislative issues within 60 days of an election. The decision usefully prunes back one tentacle of the McCain-Feingold law. But the bulk of over 400 pages of FEC regulations remains intact. The opinion has no effect on the law under which Norm Feck faces prosecution, or the regulations that frustrate other Norm Fecks across the country.

Other important sources of influence include academia and Hollywood, both tilting to the left—and both left alone by the reformers.

All Americans Do Not Have an Equal Voice

Campaign finance reform neatly accomplishes Democrats' goal of muffling political speech on the Right. Reformers seldom state that goal explicitly, of course; instead, they claim that reform gets rid of the political corruption that supposedly follows from large campaign contributions. Yet study after study shows that contributions play little or no role in how politicians vote. One of the most comprehensive [studies], conducted by a group of MIT [Massachusetts Institute of Technology] scholars in 2004, concluded that "indicators of party, ideology and district preferences account for most of the systematic variation in legislators' roll call voting behavior." The studies [align] with common sense. Most politicians enter the public arena because they hold strong beliefs on public policy. Truly corrupt pols—the Duke Cunninghams [U.S. Representative from California] of the world—want illegal bribes, not campaign donations.

Reformers also often claim to seek something more radical than eradicating corruption: equalizing political influence. During the debate over McCain-Feingold, numerous members of Congress repeatedly picked up on the "equality" theme. "It is time to let all our citizens have an equal voice," argued Georgia congressman John Lewis, a Democrat. Missouri senator Jean Carnahan, another Democrat, complained that "special interests have an advantage over average, hard-working citizens." Susan Collins, the liberal Republican senator from Maine, wanted "all Americans [to] have an equal voice."

Liberal Influence Unchecked

Yet political influence comes in many shapes, and campaign finance reformers have little interest in equalizing all of them. Take, for example, large foundations—a major source of political influence. The assets of liberal foundations such as Carnegie, Ford, and MacArthur dwarf those of their conservative counterparts: Ford's assets top $10 billion, MacArthur's $4 billion, [whereas] the Right's giant, the Bradley Foundation, commands just $500 million. Campaign finance reform leaves foundations untouched.

Other important sources of influence include academia and Hollywood, both tilting to the left—and both left alone by the reformers. Consider how the law applied to Michael Moore's anti-[George W.] Bush film *Fahrenheit 9/11* [referring to the terrorist attacks of 2001] and to competing conservative films released in the run-up to the 2004 election. A number of complaints filed with the FEC charged Moore and others with campaign finance violations; both the movie and the advertising surrounding it, the complaints asserted, amounted to illegal contributions to the [John] Kerry campaign. Despite Moore's public statements that he'd made his movie to help defeat Bush, the FEC dismissed all the complaints, noting, among other things, that the film was a commercial rather than a political effort.

But when the conservative organization Citizens United tried to release a film responding to many of *Fahrenheit 9/11*'s anti-Bush assertions, the FEC advised it that any public broadcast or advertising close to the election would be subject to McCain-Feingold regulations. Similarly, when Second Amendment activist David Hardy sought to release a movie [favoring gun rights and portraying President George W. Bush favorably] before the election ... the FEC ruled that campaign finance restrictions applied. In both cases, the FEC based its conclusion on the fact that the conservative producers, unlike Moore, weren't normally in the movie business.

Campaign finance regulation, far from improving our democratic processes, has already begun to undermine them in a number of ways.

Then there's the press—and who would deny that it has great political influence? Nevertheless, campaign finance reform leaves it unregulated thus far. More than that: as restrictions on private campaign spending grow, the free coverage that politicians get from the press becomes more and more important. And that coverage, especially coverage by the national press corps, regularly demonstrates a leftward bias, as many studies have shown. During the 2004 presidential race, the press didn't remind Americans about John Kerry's harsh criticisms of his fellow soldiers in Vietnam, or pose questions about the nature of his military service; neither did it dwell on President [George W.] Bush's strong post-9/11 leadership.

Those tasks, it's worth noting, were left to two conservative political organizations, Swift Boat Veterans for Truth and Progress for America, whose highly effective campaign ads engaged in the kind of political speech that campaign finance reform chokes.

Which sources of influence are regulated and which are not is a choice deeply entangled with tacit assumptions about who benefits from each of those sources. Despite their noble-sounding claims, reformers aren't really trying to equalize political influence: in fact, they're doing exactly the opposite, regulating only those sources of influence that they disagree with. . . .

Rules to Support Those in Power

Campaign finance regulation, far from improving our democratic processes, has already begun to undermine them in a number of ways. One is the way that it entrenches incumbents in office. Dissenting in *McConnell v. FEC*, the case that upheld the constitutionality of McCain-Feingold, [Supreme Court] Justice Antonin Scalia went to the core of the issue: "Is it accidental, do you think, that incumbents raise about three times as much 'hard money'—the sort of funding generally *not* restricted by this legislation—as do their challengers?" he scoffed. Scalia also pointed out that McCain-Feingold allowed higher contributions to candidates running against self-financed millionaires—who tend to be incumbents, [as] self-financed millionaires are usually mavericks challenging established politicians. Moreover, McCain-Feingold severely limited funding for national parties—which, Scalia wrote, are "more likely to assist cash-strapped challengers than flush-with-hard-money incumbents." "Those who have power will create election rules that maximize the likelihood that they will win reelection," the Cato Institute's Samples says. "Campaign finance laws might be, in other words, a form of corruption."

A still more insidious problem than incumbents' self-dealing is the way that campaign finance regulation discourages true grassroots political activity. Longtime Washington campaign finance attorney Jan Baran jokes that McCain-Feingold's official acronym, "BCRA," stands not for "Bipartisan Campaign Reform Act" but for "Before Campaigning, Retain Attorney." Samples adds, more seriously: "Today no one should exercise his First Amendment rights without advice from counsel, preferably one schooled in the intricacies of campaign finance regulation."

Consider two examples. During the 2000 presidential race, four men placed a homemade sign, reading VOTE REPUBLICAN: NOT AL GORE SOCIALISM, on a cotton trailer along a Texas highway. The FEC spent nearly 18 months investigating the incident, because the sign lacked the legally required information about who had paid for it. And in 2004, NASCAR driver Kirk Shelmerdine spent $50 to affix a BUSH-CHENEY '04 decal to an unsold spot on his car's advertising space. The FEC admonished him for making an unreported campaign expenditure. Such cases are not merely examples of bureaucratic excess, points out campaign finance lawyer Bob Bauer, a lonely antireform voice in Democratic circles: under today's intrusive laws, Shelmerdine's activities *ought* to have set off an FEC inquiry. . . .

Another disturbing regulatory trend is to go beyond regulating the money that funds speech to regulating the speech itself.

Though they claim to speak for average citizens, reformers don't care much about the way their reforms hurt those citizens. Trevor Potter, president of the Campaign Legal Center and a McCain adviser, has dismissed complaints by arguing that campaign finance laws are no more complex than antitrust or patent laws. "They are worth the inconvenience and lawyers' fees they generate," says Potter—who also heads the campaign finance practice at the upscale law firm of Caplin & Drysdale, where partner billing rates can range upward of $750 per hour.

Creating a Web of Regulation

Despite the labyrinthine complexity of campaign finance law, the reform community is busily expanding regulation even further. For example, the FEC's regulations implementing McCain-Feingold specifically exempted much Web activity from regulation. So the law's lead House sponsors, Democrat Marty Meehan of Massachusetts and Republican Chris Shays of Connecticut, sued successfully in federal court to force the FEC to regulate more Web activity, and then defeated a congressional effort to codify an Internet exemption to the law. The ensuing FEC rules took a light hand, but the troubling fact remains that individual online activity is now subject to regulation.

Another disturbing regulatory trend is to go beyond regulating the money that funds speech to regulating the speech itself. For example, in the Shelmerdine case, the FEC valued the driver's "contribution" not at the $50 that it cost him to place a decal on his car, but at several thousand dollars—what the FEC determined to be the advertising spot's monetary value. Similarly, if an executive instructs his secretary to type a fund-raising letter, the FEC values the contribution not at the cost of typing the letter, but at the amount of money that the letter raises. This move dramatically expands the reach of campaign finance laws: not only can the FEC limit funds that can be used for speech, but it can limit speech itself by assigning it a monetary value. And it opens the door to all kinds of mischief: for instance, the FEC could determine that a posting on a popular blog was worth thousands of dollars.

If that sounds farfetched, consider that in Washington State a trial court ordered that radio disc jockeys John Carlson and Kirby Wilbur report their on-air talk as campaign contributions. The Washington State Supreme Court reversed the case this April [2007], but the court didn't base its decision on the First Amendment[, however, and instead ruled] that the statute in question didn't cover radio talk. In a footnote, the court specifically noted that "nothing in our decision today forecloses the legislature, or the people via the initiative process, from limiting the statutory media exemption."

Such an intrusive regulatory regime is but a logical step toward the holy grail [a goal long sought and widely believed to be unattainable] of campaign finance reform: a fully regulated, taxpayer-funded system of political speech. Richard Hasen, an oft-quoted expert on campaign finance whom the media regularly portray as a moderate voice for reform, has proposed [both] limiting citizens' financial participation in politics to a government-provided voucher and prohibiting any other private funding of political speech. Edward Foley, a former Ohio state solicitor and director of Ohio State University's influential election-law program, has made a similar proposal. Both experts would extend their regulations even to newspaper editorial pages. Hasen explains that he's trying to solve the "Rupert Murdoch problem" [referring to a typically conservative media mogul]—just in case you had any doubt about whom he's got in his sights.

The Courts Cannot Solve the Problem Alone

Conservatives, historically uninterested in mobilizing against "reform," have tended to depend on the courts to strike down the worst laws. Indeed, many believe that President [George W.] Bush signed McCain-Feingold because his legal advisers assured him that the courts would never tolerate the law's new restrictions. But the Supreme Court has been erratic in protecting political speech. In *McConnell v. FEC*, the case that upheld McCain-Feingold, the Court gave political speech less protection than Internet pornography, simulated child pornography, topless dancing, tobacco advertising, and the dissemination of illegally acquired information.

It seems doubtful that the Court will ever take a stand against campaign finance regulation in full.

Last term, the Supreme Court did step back from the abyss. In *Randall v. Sorrell*, it struck down expenditure limits and very low contribution limits (including limits on volunteer time) in Vermont[;] in *Wisconsin Right to Life v. FEC*, it held that there might be constitutionally necessitated exceptions to McCain-Feingold's limits on broadcast ads mentioning a candidate within 60 days of an election. (The latter case will be back before the Court this term, since a lower court has held that Wisconsin Right to Life's ad indeed merited such an exception.)

These are encouraging developments, but free-speech advocates shouldn't count too heavily on the [Supreme Court justices] to do the heavy lifting. The main reason that the Court decided last term's cases differently from *McConnell* is that Justice [Samuel] Alito had replaced Justice [Sandra Day] O'Connor, giving the Court a 5–4 majority in favor of a more robust interpretation of the First Amendment. But two members of that majority are over age 70. It is unlikely that President Bush will get another judicial appointment; it is equally unlikely that a Democratic president, or a President McCain, would appoint pro-speech judges to the Court.

It also seems doubtful that the Court will ever take a stand against campaign finance regulation in toto [as a whole]. Justice [Anthony] Kennedy, part of the 5–4 pro-speech majority, is a staunch supporter of free speech in individual cases, but unlike Justices Scalia and [Clarence] Thomas, he has been unwilling to hold that all contribution limits are unconstitutional. Absent a clear constitutional bar to regulation, a future

Court may remove whatever restraints this Court places on the legislature—much as the *McConnell* Court did to *Buckley*'s curbs on FECA.

"I have come to doubt that the masses of the people have sense enough to govern themselves," wrote Ben Tillman, the founder of federal campaign finance reform, in 1916. Eighty years later, House Minority Leader Richard Gephardt famously described the battle over campaign finance reform as "two important values in direct conflict: freedom of speech and our desire for healthy campaigns in a healthy democracy. You can't have both."

Many a tax- and regulation-prone politician, stymied by real political debate, would agree with both men. But Norm Feck and his Parker North neighbors, Washington deejays Carlson and Wilbur . . . and tens of thousands of NASCAR fans realize that free speech is not a bar to healthy democracy but a cornerstone of it. It's imperative that we speak up to defend freedom of speech—before that very speaking up becomes impossible.

5

Campaign Finance Reform Does Not Stifle Political Free Speech

V.B. Price

A member of the faculty at the University of New Mexico's University Honors Program, V.B. Price is a teacher of poetry and Greek and Roman literature. He is also a writer and local columnist in the Albuquerque area.

The Bipartisan Campaign Reform Act of 2002 (also known as the McCain-Feingold Act) sought to limit the power of big money in political advertising. Since the passage of the law, conservatives have attempted to overturn it on the presumption that curbing political ads is a violation of free speech. This argument is fallacious, though. Political propaganda is designed to obscure issues and smear candidates; it is not a venue for clear, credible debate. To keep obtrusive misinformation out of the political sphere—where free speech should reign—campaign finance reform measures must triumph over corporate power-brokering.

When it came to being persuasive, credibility used to be the guiding principle. If an orator, a philosopher, or a politician wasn't credible, he wasn't convincing either. Credibility was based on character, intelligence, integrity, knowledge, and, most of all, on independence.

Only free individual human beings, or advocates for the rights of individuals, can have authentic credibility. When we

V.B. Price, "Propaganda Does Not Equal Free Speech," *The New Mexico Independent*, September 9, 2009. Reproduced by permission of the author.

don't think for ourselves, however, we become political dummies for the ventriloquism of ideologues and the propaganda of their secretive rich sponsors.

Organizations of all kinds [that] assert their right to "free speech," equating persuasion with money and the mind tricks of the advertising that money can buy, have no credibility.

Who in his right mind believes political advertising? All anyone has to do is consider the source.

Political Propaganda Masquerading as Free Speech

The differences between free speech and propaganda will be an unspoken part of a heated debate before the [U.S.] Supreme Court this week [in September 2009], when it begins hearing arguments on a case called *Citizens United v. Federal Election Commission*. At issue will be the supposed First Amendment rights of corporate and other legal entities to spend all the money they want opposing or supporting political candidates with direct political advertising. [The high court ruled on this case in 2010 that restrictions on the speech of corporations and unions are unconstitutional.]

Commercial propaganda techniques put to the service of political viewpoints clutter up the marketplace of ideas. And yet both the business community and constitutional watchdogs like the ACLU [American Civil Liberties Union] support the basic idea that spending money freely is analogous to speaking freely.

The Cato Institute, a libertarian think tank, calls campaign finance regulation "thought control." But that, of course, puts big money not only in the category of speech, but of thought. And that's incredible and dismissible. Groups don't think or speak. They mouth what they are told to, or what they, as a whole, have agreed upon. And there is always a question as to how an agreement was reached and by whom, and who believes in it or merely acquiesces to it.

The Supreme Court could overturn numerous laws evolved over decades that keep corporations and unions from directly funding political ads. At issue is a film called *Hillary: The Movie*, a blatant piece of political propaganda directed against the presidential candidacy of Hillary Clinton and produced by Citizens United, a right wing political group. Who funds Citizens United is hard to find out. Is it a front group for some mighty big money, for corporate money, for pro-fascists, for some church? It's all left up to the imagination. They are a 501-c3, however, and are tax exempt. But if you don't know where the money is coming from, no one should take the propaganda seriously. And propaganda, itself, should never be taken at face value.

Lumping group speak with individual speech as it's protected by the First Amendment is intellectually specious.

In June [2009], when the Supreme Court first heard arguments in the *Hillary* case, it decided to expand the inquiry and to use the case as a platform from which to explore the whole concept of campaign advertising restrictions, rather than base judgment on the case brought before it. This is flagrant "judicial activism," a term used normally against liberal justices. But this strange and irregular broadening of the case is a conservative notion, as far as the court is concerned.

Group Speak Often Lacks Credibility

Lumping group speak with individual speech as it's protected by the First Amendment is intellectually specious.

Only individuals have the ability to think for themselves, to weigh arguments and evidence, and to even change their minds. Only individuals have the capacity for true independence, to go against their own specific interests, let's say, for the good of all. Only individuals can make such sacrifices. Corporations don't. Labor Unions don't. Political parties, public and private lobbyists, and experts for hire do not. Their independence must always be questioned. They invariably allow ends to justify means, and [they] often employ any means, short of murder, to make their point. More troubling, [though] wealthy persons might avail themselves of the expertise of a public relations [PR] company to do their thinking for them, most of them do not. And even the wealthy often think and speak impromptu [without preparation]. Group speak is almost invariably PR speak. And that lacks, almost invariably, any credibility whatsoever.

That's why free speech is the inalienable right of human beings, not "juristic persons," a concept unknown to the First Amendment of the Constitution. Speech and thought are individual human attributes. Legal entities can only "speak" across a spectrum of propaganda. Truth is not in their purview [ways of seeing or knowing]. They have no character, no conscience, no soul. All they have is a lot of money, which buys them the chance at a lot of power.

If group speakers are allow[ed] to hide their [identities] and create infomercials that purport to be the truth, then confusion and misinformation will utterly corrupt elections in America.

Consequences of Undoing Campaign Finance Reform

If the Supreme Court overturns the McCain-Feingold [that is, the Bipartisan Campaign Reform Act] restrictions on unlimited political advertising by corporations, unions, and other group speakers, there would [be] an array of interesting implications, some of which include:

- The unintended consequences of group speakers who go against those who brought them to the dance. Corporations, in particular, are loyal to no political party.

45

They could turn [against] Republicans and conservatives as fast as they've turned against liberals while covertly supporting Democratic corporate Clintonistas [supporters of 2008 presidential candidate Hillary Clinton], or as fast as they've turned against blather mouth Glen[n] Beck [a conservative radio and television host].

- If group speakers are required to identify themselves in their advertising (as in "this piece of biased balderdash is brought to you by Slick Oil"), then voters can make their own assessment of credibility. If group speakers are allow[ed] to hide their [identities] and create infomercials that purport to be the truth, then confusion and misinformation will utterly corrupt elections in America. Many of us already suspect our election system is rigged.

- If restrictions on group speakers funding political ads [are] lifted, then local businesses, local groups, local unions—local associations of all kinds—could also fund ad campaigns for or against specific candidates. An advertising campaign is much more potent than a mere endorsement. But endorsements keep voters away from [a candidate] as much as they draw them in. And a vicious ad campaign can backfire.

- If the Supreme Court abandons all campaign finance restrictions without requiring that sponsors take credit for the ads, then the often savage recklessness that anonymity breeds among those who comment on the Internet will descend upon local, as well as national, politics, and infect it with the brutal drivel that people spew when they are not held accountable for what they say.

Only individuals and groups who identify themselves have a chance at being credible. That's why the murky anonymity of the backers of Citizens United casts a pall on the validity of the *Hillary* suit itself. Why did the Supreme Court choose this particular case to reexamine campaign advertising restrictions in general? Has the court's conservative majority been corrupted by invisible corporate forces?

6

Free Speech Is No Basis for Undoing the Bipartisan Campaign Reform Act

Jeffrey Rosen

Jeffrey Rosen is a professor of law at George Washington University in Washington, D.C. He is a frequent contributor to the New York Times, Atlantic Monthly, *and National Public Radio and is the author of* The Supreme Court: The Personalities and Rivalries That Defined America.

The Bipartisan Campaign Reform Act of 2002 (also known as the McCain-Feingold Act) has been effective at keeping candidates for public office from receiving soft-money contributions from advocacy organizations and wealthy individuals. The law, therefore, has done much to thwart the corruption of candidates who otherwise might pursue the agendas of their wealthiest backers. Although critics of this reform measure have argued that curtailing money and advertisements (which are chiefly bought with campaign funds) are infringements on free speech, it is difficult to accept that eliminating limits on soft-money contributions would ensure free elections. To overturn McCain-Feingold on the merits of a free speech debate is wrongheaded and would simply turn electioneering into a contest of wealth and corporate interests.

American democracy has always been haunted by the specter of concentrated wealth. How can the principle of one man, one vote be honored when the accumulation of dollars

Jeffrey Rosen, "The Right to Spend," *New York Times Magazine*, July 8, 2007, p. 11. Copyright © 2007 by The New York Times Company. Reprinted with permission.

translates so readily into the accumulation of political influence? If all citizens enjoy the equal right to participate in politics with their wallets, is it possible to hold a fair election? In today's [2007] proudly money-mad, winner-take-all economy, these questions are as urgent as ever. The spending patterns of the very rich help form our consumer habits and fill the pages of our magazines; it's little wonder that they shape our politics as well. The ongoing presidential campaign often seems to be a (somewhat) glorified competition for cash, and when a billionaire contemplates a candidacy, the entire process comes to a halt.

The McCain-Feingold act [also known as the Bipartisan Campaign Reform Act], passed in 2002, was meant to do something about this; it was meant to even the balance between democracy and money. By limiting the donation of unregulated "soft" money to political parties and banning "issue ads" in the buildup to an election, [the act] made it harder for a small number of wealthy donors to dominate the political process. Now, however, the Supreme Court has used the First Amendment to throw out one part of the law [which limited campaign ads posted within 60 days of the election] and threatened to discard the rest [in 2010 the high court ruled the act's restriction of union and corporate speech to be unconstitutional]. In this new gilded age, are we doomed to return to gilded-age politics?

Banning soft money has forced the parties and candidates to learn to raise money from individuals who are not among the superrich.

Certainly, the end of McCain-Feingold would have consequences. The ban on soft money addressed a serious political problem about wealth and political access: more than half of the $500 million in soft money raised in 2000 came from only 800 donors, each contributing a minimum of $120,000. Fully 435 of them were corporations or unions, and the rest were among the wealthiest 1 percent of individual citizens. Under McCain-Feingold, the influence of those donors has been reduced. Despite the rise of so-called 527 organizations [Named after a section of the U.S. tax code, 527 organizations are political groups that avoid regulation by the Federal Election Commission and thus are not restricted in the size of their campaign contributions because they supposedly do not support candidates directly but merely endorse specific issues or mobilize voter turnout at the polls. Critics often charge that 527 organizations do not maintain the proper separation from candidate advocacy demanded by the tax law.] to exploit loopholes in the law, the ban on corporate soft-money contributions to political parties has had some success. Candidates are relieved that they do not have to help solicit corporate soft money, as they did during the fund-raising scandals of the go-go [unrestrained] '90s, and corporations are relieved at not being shaken down to contribute to both parties to hedge their bets. More important, banning soft money has forced the parties and candidates to learn to raise money from individuals who are not among the superrich, and the Internet has allowed them to do so in cost-effective ways. In the first half of 2007, Barack Obama received contributions from more than 250,000 individuals while raising millions over the Internet.

[If the courts overturned McCain-Feingold] the effects of wealth would once more be magnified as the size of donations ballooned.

The Impact of Overturning the Bipartisan Campaign Reform Act

But the [Supreme Court Justice John G.] Roberts Court may not allow the ban on soft money to stand for long. Although four liberal justices, following the thinking of [Justice] Stephen Breyer, have concluded that campaign-finance laws serve the purposes of the First Amendment by enhancing public confidence in democracy and equalizing political participation, four conservative justices have reached the opposite conclusion on the grounds that giving money is a form of speech. And Chief Justice Roberts may well join them in a future case. So let's imagine that the court votes before long to strike down the ban on soft money, gutting what remains of McCain-Feingold. What would American politics look like then?

In some ways, it would look a lot like American politics before the 1970s. Corporations would give freely to state and national parties. The effects of wealth would once more be magnified as the size of donations ballooned. But not all of the effects of radical deregulation would be negative. Mega-rich candidates would face better-financed rivals and thus inspire less fear. And, having discovered the virtues of Internet fund-raising, candidates are unlikely to ignore small donors, as they did in the '90s.

The most significant result of a decision to strike down virtually all campaign-finance regulations would be to dash reformers' hopes for more comprehensive reform—hope, that is, for the sort of policies that proponents of equal access in politics believe would actually work. In Belgium, for example, parties receive 85 percent of their revenue from the government, and spending is strictly restricted during the three months before an election. Such an approach, however, would be hard to reconcile with Americans' dislike of subsidizing politicians—or with our First Amendment tradition, whether interpreted by the [1953–69 Earl] Warren Court or the Roberts Court.

A Free Speech Victory Might Lead to Unfair Elections

The larger question, of course, is whether it's useful for the country to have yet another polarized debate about whether giving money is free speech. The truth is that few people are absolutists on the question. No less an egalitarian than the political theorist Michael Walzer, who supports a "radical ban on private fund-raising," has suggested that candidates should at least be allowed to hold bake sales. And free-speech conservatives, who care more about liberty than equality in the political process, haven't yet questioned the ban on direct corporate contributions to candidates, which dates back to the Progressive era [c. 1880–1920]. Since 1976, the Supreme Court has tried to finesse this debate. It has insisted that Congress can regulate contributions to candidates more extensively than expenditures by candidates, because contributions are more likely to lead to quid pro quo corruption and are less central to free expression. But now the court seems on the verge of throwing out this nuanced position and announcing that because money is almost always speech, it can almost never be regulated. That's a plausible vision of the First Amendment, but whether it will produce a political system that inspires confidence among the American people remains to be seen.

7

The Supreme Court Was Right to Overturn the Millionaire's Amendment

Hans A. von Spakovsky

Hans A. von Spakovsky is a former commissioner on the Federal Election Commission and a former counsel to the Assistant Attorney General for Civil Rights at the Justice Department.

The Millionaire's Amendment to the Bipartisan Campaign Reform Act of 2002 permitted a candidate seeking public office to receive triple the standard contribution limit from supporters if the candidate's opponent was a wealthy individual who self-financed his or her campaign. Although this amendment was meant to level the playing field, it violates free speech by giving candidates running against self-financed opponents an unfair leg up in disseminating their ideas. The amendment also requires self-financed candidates to report how their money is spent, whereas their opponents are under no such obligation. Most dangerously, though, it empowers Congress to influence how speech enters the marketplace of ideas—establishing a dangerous precedent that could be used to extend such powers into other realms of public debate.

In the excitement over the Supreme Court's decision in the [Washington] D.C. gun ban case, almost overlooked was a second decision that struck another blow against the McCain-Feingold federal campaign finance law. In *Davis v. FEC* [Federal Election Commission], a 5–4 majority found the "Millionaire's Amendment" to be unconstitutional, holding that it imposed an unprecedented penalty on any candidate who robustly exercises his First Amendment rights by requiring him to choose between the right to engage in unfettered political speech or to be subject to discriminatory fundraising limitations. This was a significant decision reaffirming First Amendment principles and rejecting a new and dangerous justification for campaign restrictions.

The 2002 Millionaire's Amendment tripled the $2,300 contribution limit for a federal candidate facing a self-financed opponent who spent more than $350,000 of his own funds. It also lifted the limit on money spent by the political party on behalf of the candidate who was not self-funded, while imposing substantial reporting requirements on his freespending opponent. At first blush, this would seem like a good change in the law to everyone who believes that the current contribution limit of $2,300 is too low and that the party coordination limits make no sense since political parties are supposed to help elect their candidates. The problem, however, was the rationale used by Congress for this amendment.

A Dangerous Precedent

Starting with the *Buckley* [*v. Valeo* (1976)] decision 30 years ago, the Supreme Court has approved campaign finance laws that regulate and restrict contributions and political activity on the basis that they prevent corruption or the appearance of corruption. [Because] the Millionaire's Amendment raised the contribution limit, it obviously could not be justified on that basis. If limiting contributions to $2,300 is necessary to avoid corrupting a candidate, then allowing $6,900 to be contributed would pose a much greater danger. Instead, Congress justified this provision on egalitarian grounds—it was required to level the playing field and reduce the "natural" advantage that wealthy candidates have in campaigns for federal office.

The danger of this rationale is that it could be used by Congress to justify almost any restriction on political speech, political activity, and electoral campaigns. Fortunately, a majority of the Court led by Justice [Samuel] Alito recognized the complete fallacy of this argument. As Justice Alito wrote, "[t]he argument that a candidate's speech may be restricted in order to 'level electoral opportunities' has ominous implications because it would permit Congress to arrogate the voters' authority to evaluate the strengths of candidates competing for office." Alito concluded that no interest in leveling electoral opportunities for candidates of different personal wealth could justify the asymmetrical contribution limits imposed by the Millionaire's Amendment.

The fact that four justices of the U.S. Supreme Court would actually assert that there is nothing wrong with limiting the amount of political speech engaged in during an election is shocking.

The Court also threw out the disclosure requirements since it found the basic provision of the law unconstitutional, a holding that has other implications. Last year [in 2007], the Supreme Court found the electioneering communications provision of McCain-Feingold unconstitutional. This provision had banned certain advertisements that named a federal candidate even if the ad had nothing to do with an upcoming election, such as an issue ad urging a senator to vote a particular way on upcoming legislation. However, when the FEC implemented this exemption with a new regulation in November [2007], it still imposed a disclosure requirement. I was the only commissioner on the FEC who opposed this regulation because the agency had no authority to require disclosure of activity that the Supreme Court had found the FEC had no power to regulate. The holding in *Davis* makes it clear that this regulation is unconstitutional. The newly approved commissioners on the FEC should promptly eliminate it.

Free Speech Should Not Be Limited

The most disturbing aspect of the *Davis* case is the dissenting opinion written by Justice [John Paul] Stevens. Stevens believes that leveling the political playing field represents a "modest, sensible, and plainly constitutional" basis for congressional action. The fact that it would limit political speech "would likely have the salutary effect of improving the quality of the exposition of ideas." He says that it would be better if political campaigns were conducted in a more "orderly" manner such as oral argument before the Supreme Court since that produces "high-value" speech: "flooding the airwaves with slogans and sound-bites may well do more to obscure the issues than to enlighten listeners." Unbelievably, Stevens posits that in elections, "the notion that rules limiting the quantity of speech are just as offensive to the First Amendment as rules limiting the content of speech is plainly incorrect."

The fact that four justices of the U.S. Supreme Court would actually assert that there is nothing wrong with limiting the amount of political speech engaged in during an election is shocking. It is scary to think of such a constitutional doctrine becoming accepted precedent if just one justice had switched his vote. It graphically illustrates just how important the next president's appointments to the Supreme Court will be to preserving our First Amendment rights in the political arena.

8

Overturning the Millionaire's Amendment Weakened Democracy

Jay Mandle

Jay Mandle is a professor of economics at Colgate University in New York. He is the author of Democracy, America, and the Age of Globalization.

The Supreme Court was correct in eliminating the double standards inherent in the Millionaire's Amendment to the Bipartisan Campaign Reform Act. This part of the law unjustly stipulated that candidates for public office who ran against wealthy opponents could receive larger donations from supporters to even the playing field in campaign spending. In reaching its decision, however, the court strongly suggested that regulation of any kind on wealthy candidates would not be tolerable under First Amendment principles. Such a presumption is unwarranted because it closes the door on further reform, though the conclusion is clear that something must be done to redress the unfair advantage wealth confers in political campaigning.

The power of wealth in the political process was endorsed last week [in June 2008] by the [U.S.] Supreme Court. Its decision to strike down the "Millionaire's Amendment" to the Bipartisan Campaign [Reform] Act (BCRA) was all but overlooked because of the media's attention to the Court's [Washington] DC handgun decision. But the majority opinion, writ-

Jay Mandle, "The Millionaire's Amendment," The Huffington Post, July 3, 2008. Reproduced by permission.

ten by Justice Samuel Alito in the case known as *Davis v. Federal Election Commission*, may have even more profound long-term consequences than the overthrow of Washington's gun law.

This decision was handed down hard on the heels of Senator [Barack] Obama's rejecting public funds in the general election. It is the latest evidence of what looks like a disturbing trend reinforcing the pervasive role of big money in American political life.

The provision ruled unconstitutional by the Court was designed to prevent a "millionaire"—someone who spent more than $350,000 of his or her personal funds—from buying an election with personal funds. Under the Amendment's terms, limits on campaign donations had been relaxed for a candidate facing a "millionaire" opponent who had contributed more than a specified amount to his or her own campaign. The intent was to reduce the political advantage of personal wealth.

The majority [of Supreme Court Justices] actually argued—contrary to a vast amount of scholarship and common sense—that wealth was not important politically.

The Court Ignored the Unfair Advantage of Wealth

Admittedly, the Millionaire's Amendment, as written, was constitutionally flawed. It [relaxed] contribution limits for a millionaire's opponents but not for the millionaire, thereby establishing a double standard: self-funded candidates were faced with more demanding contribution restrictions than donation-funded candidates. The Court rejected this mechanism. Its view was that the double standard effectively violated the First Amendment because it conferred an unfair "fund-raising advantage for opponents in the competitive context of electoral politics."

The Court was right to reject different contribution limits for competing candidates. It would not take much to turn such a provision to partisan advantage. But unfortunately, the Court did not stop there. The 5–4 majority opinion went beyond the question of differing contribution rules. It used the occasion to question whether any form of a Millionaire's Amendment would be constitutionally acceptable, strongly hinting that it would not be.

The majority actually argued—contrary to a vast amount of scholarship and common sense—that wealth was not important politically. "Different candidates have different strengths." Writing for the majority, Justice [Samuel] Alito claimed that wealth is on a par with having "the benefit of a well-known family name" or being a celebrity.

This trivializes the role of wealth in politics. The fact of the matter is that it takes vast amounts of money to become a successful candidate. Virtually no one can be elected to office without either being rich or having access to wealthy donors. Funders exercise substantial leverage in determining political outcomes.

Lack of Regulation Undermines Democracy

The fundamental question here is whether a commitment to democracy requires that the political system be designed to maximize political equality. Should the mayor of New York or the governor of New Jersey be able to overwhelm [his] opponents with vast personal fortunes?

Alito in effect says, "Yes." Indeed, he comes very close to saying that it is impermissible for the Congress to make rules to achieve the kind of electoral equality that BCRA sought. In his words, Congress should refrain from "making judgments" about the extent to which factors such as private financing should be permitted to influence the electoral process. "It is a dangerous business," he writes, "for Congress to use the election laws to influence the voters' choices."

But it is just as dangerous to abandon rules to limit the influence private wealth [has] on elections as it is to overreach in the opposite direction, as the Millionaire's Amendment did. All election systems require rules and legal limits; those rules cannot help but influence political outcomes. But the absence of regulations restricting wealthy, self-financing candidates undermines democracy. The Court's ruling in effect affirms the power of the rich.

This is a worrisome sign. The tone of the opinion suggests that even if the double standard problem had been corrected, the Court would have found a reason to rule against the Millionaire's Amendment. If this [case] is an indication of how this Court will rule on the influence of big money on elections, it points to a formidable barrier to strengthening our democracy.

9

The Ban on Nonprofit Campaign Spending Should Be Overturned

Stuart Taylor, Jr.

Stuart Taylor, Jr. is a fellow at the Brookings Institution, a public policy think tank. He is a contributing editor for Newsweek *and a columnist for the* National Journal.

The Bipartisan Campaign Reform Act of 2002 barred most organizations from funding candidates for public office. The rationale was clear: Big businesses could buy enough advertising for their candidate to swamp the message of poorly funded opponents. Although this ban makes sense regarding corporate enterprises that represent various stockholders who may not collectively endorse a single candidate, the restriction is illogical when applied to nonprofit organizations. In weighing campaign finance reforms, the U.S. Supreme Court should recognize that nonprofit organizations are advocacy groups that unite behind specific issues and candidates. The court should thus remove the ban on nonprofit campaign spending while keeping for-profit, corporate influence out of public elections.

In an unusual, relatively unpublicized June 29 [2009] order, the [U.S.] Supreme Court scheduled a special oral argument for September 9 [2009] to consider using a pending case to sweep away the 62-year-old ban on independent corporate spending to influence elections.

That would be the Court's biggest attack ever on campaign finance laws. It would also be a big mistake. There is no good reason to empower Big Business CEOs [chief executive officers] to influence elections by spending other people's money—by which I mean money belonging to ideologically eclectic shareholders, most of whom do not want it invested in election campaigns.

But for all the alarums [uproar] among liberal election-law experts, I doubt that the Court's majority is planning to open the floodgates to unlimited campaign spending by Big Business.

Loosen Restrictions on Nonprofits

I am guessing, and hoping, that the justices will instead use the pending case, *Citizens United v. Federal Election Commission [FEC]*, to draw a principled, pragmatic, nonideological line between business corporations and nonprofit advocacy corporations.

Such a decision would uphold the First Amendment rights of citizen groups to spend their individual members' dues and contributions to support or oppose federal candidates, as long as they don't serve as conduits for money amassed in the economic marketplace by business corporations.

[Whereas] many conservatives are all too eager to unleash Big Business to spend on campaigns, most liberals have been all too content to censor nonprofit advocacy corporations. They have also ignored the blatantly self-interested and illegitimate nature of Congress's decision to draft the campaign finance restrictions so broadly as to hog-tie such advocacy groups, as described below.

The result has been to make it a crime for incorporated citizens groups such as the Sierra Club, the National Rifle Association, organizations supporting and opposing abortion rights, and many [other] large and small nonprofits to pool the contributions and dues of like-minded members and spend them to support or oppose federal candidates.

Almost all such groups find it necessary to incorporate, for liability limitation and other reasons. But that's no reason to deny them their First Amendment rights to free speech or "to petition the government for a redress of grievances," which [rights] were clearly intended to protect collective as well as individual political activities.

The reason that most business corporations (and unions) have properly been barred from making independent expenditures to influence elections is that it would distort the democratic process.

Twisted Logic

The unfairness of barring campaign spending by these nonprofits is underscored by the fact that some big corporations—such as General Electric (which owns NBC [The National Broadcasting Corporation]), other broadcast and cable networks, Rupert Murdoch's News Corp., and *The New York Times*—are exempted from campaign finance laws because they are, or own, media corporations. George Soros and other wealthy individuals also have First Amendment rights to spend unlimited sums of their own money in campaigns.

The reason that most business corporations (and unions) have properly been barred from making independent expenditures to influence elections is that it would distort the democratic process [and] open the door for CEOs (or union bosses) to spend vast amounts of shareholders' (or union members') money supporting or opposing candidates whom the shareholders (or members) have not meaningfully chosen to support or oppose.

But the same logic simply does not apply to nonprofits that want to spend the money of members who pay dues precisely for the purpose of promoting political causes and, in some cases, candidates.

"Nonprofit advocacy groups funded by individuals are readily distinguishable from for-profit corporations funded by general treasuries," Stanford University law professor Kathleen Sullivan explained in a friend-of-the-court brief in a somewhat analogous 2007 case. "Speech by nonprofit advocacy groups on behalf of their members does not 'corrupt' candidates or 'distort' the political marketplace. Instead, it is [campaign finance law] that distorts, leaving wealthy individuals and corporate media conglomerates unfettered in their preelection broadcast advocacy, and inducing sophisticated corporations to turn to alternatives such as PACs [political action committees], while thwarting speech by individuals of moderate means who have banded together in grassroots groups to express their views."

Sullivan was arguing for exempting nonprofit advocacy corporations from the 2002 McCain-Feingold campaign finance law's [also named the Bipartisan Campaign Reform Act] new restrictions on corporate funding of broadcast, cable, and satellite ads that purport to be "issue ads" but in fact include "electioneering." The justices ignored the business-nonprofit distinction in that case, choosing instead (by 5–4) to adopt an extremely narrow definition of electioneering.

But Sullivan's logic also argues for exempting nonprofits from the 62-year-old congressional ban on any and all corporate or union campaign spending, even if the sole purpose is to support or oppose federal candidates.

Interpreting the First Amendment

There are two exceptions to this ban—one for specially created political action committees and another for so-called MCFL corporations, named after the Court's 1986 decision in

FEC v. Massachusetts Citizens for Life. But the cost and complexity of setting up a PAC and current law's exceedingly narrow definition of MCFL corporations make those options impractical for the vast majority of nonprofit grassroots advocacy groups.

Citizens United, a conservative incorporated nonprofit group, made a movie lambasting presidential candidate Hillary Rodham Clinton; the group distributed the film online, on DVD, and in theaters. Citizens United also wanted to show the film on a cable video-on-demand service, but the FEC ruled that the law banned corporate funding of such a direct attack ad on any cable program.

In the initial briefs and during the March 24 [2009] oral arguments, the lawyer for Citizens United, Theodore Olson, urged various narrow grounds for overturning the FEC's ruling, such as holding that video-on-demand programming should not be treated as the kind of "broadcast, cable, or satellite communication" covered by McCain-Feingold.

What grabbed the justices' attention, however, was a series of admissions by the government's lawyer, Malcolm Stewart. He said that the government construes the First Amendment so narrowly as to allow Congress, if it chooses, to adopt a hypothetical ban on the financing by any corporation—with the *possible* exception of media corporations—even of books, articles, signs, or Internet postings (as well as broadcast, cable, and satellite ads) supporting or opposing federal candidates.

That seemed to shock some justices. "If we accept your constitutional argument," Chief Justice John Roberts said, "we're establishing a precedent that you yourself say would extend to banning [a] book" paid for by a corporation.

These concerns may help explain why on June 29—in a cryptic order overshadowed by publicity about the 5–4 decision upholding a reverse-discrimination lawsuit by white firefighters—the Court set *Citizens United* for reargument on September 9 [2009].

The order requested new briefs on a big, broad question: whether to overrule "either or both" *Austin v. Michigan Chamber of Commerce*, a 1990 decision upholding the 1947 ban on independent corporate campaign expenditures, and the part of the 2003 decision in *McConnell v. FEC* that upheld McCain-Feingold's ban on corporate funding of electioneering ads.

Does this mean that the five more-conservative justices are preparing to give all corporations the same rights as individuals to spend on elections? Possibly. [In January 2010 the high court ruled the McCain-Feingold restrictions on union and corporate speech to be unconstitutional.] But I'm betting that they—perhaps joined by one or more of the liberal justices—end up liberating nonprofit advocacy corporations alone.

Congress slipped a provision carefully designed to muffle ordinary citizens' criticisms of politicians into what was advertised as a restriction on political spending by Big Business and Big Labor.

Muffling the Freedom to Criticize

That would make a great deal of sense, both for the reasons explained by Sullivan and for those evident in the unsavory process by which Congress decided *not* to exempt nonprofit advocacy corporations from McCain-Feingold's electioneering provision.

I detailed in an April 28, 2007 column how many senators initially recognized that no justification existed for extending the restrictions on electioneering ads to nonprofit citizen advocacy groups—but then adopted the so-called Wellstone amendment to do just that. By railing against the "attack ads" that had been used mainly by advocacy groups, supporters of that amendment showed that their objective was to censor criticism of themselves, not to prevent corruption or limit Big Business influence.

"This bill ... is about slowing political advertising and making sure the flow of negative ads by outside interest groups does not continue to permeate the airwaves," Senator Maria Cantwell, D-Wash., said on the Senate floor, echoing the views of many.

So it was that Congress slipped a provision carefully designed to muffle ordinary citizens' criticisms of politicians into what was advertised as a restriction on political spending by Big Business and Big Labor, by making it a federal crime for *any* corporation (except media corporations) to pay for electioneering ads.

This [action] made a mockery of First Amendment rights that were intended, above all else, to guarantee citizens— acting in groups as well as individually—the freedom to criticize officeholders and candidates.

The justices can and should excise the unconstitutional Wellstone amendment while leaving the restrictions on business corporations and unions intact.

10

The Campaign Finance Decision Upholds the First Amendment

Paul Sherman

Paul Sherman is an attorney with the Institute for Justice, which litigates free speech cases throughout the nation.

The Supreme Court upheld fundamental First Amendment rights in its ruling in Citizens United v. FEC. *The ruling, which struck down federal campaign finance law restricting corporate spending in campaigns, and also reversed a previous ruling, was a victory for free speech. The* Citizens United *ruling will enliven political debate so that voters can make informed decisions.*

Supreme Court observers have been waiting a long time for the decision in *Citizens United v. FEC* [Federal Election Commission], the *"Hillary: The Movie case"* that was first argued last March [2009], reargued in September, and finally decided today [January 21, 2010]. For fans of the First Amendment, it was worth the wait.

First, some background. During the 2008 election, the nonprofit group Citizens United wanted to make a film available on cable-on-demand that was critical of then-candidate Hillary Clinton. But because Citizens United is organized as a corporation, its speech was banned under the McCain-Feingold campaign-finance law. Citizens United challenged this ban, and on Thursday, Jan. 21, 2010, the U.S. Supreme Court handed down its ruling, striking down this provision of McCain-Feingold and reversing a previous ruling—*Austin v. Michigan Chamber of Commerce*—that permitted the government to ban corporations and labor unions from promoting or opposing political candidates.

Reformers are not content to leave something as important as election results to voter free will.

The ruling represents a tremendous victory for free speech and a serious blow to proponents of campaign-finance "reform," who have roundly denounced the ruling and have all but predicted the downfall of the Republic as a result. But the reformers' rhetoric is just that; the Court's ruling will simply result in a more diverse mix of political speech, and that is a good thing for American democracy.

The ruling in Citizens United is a straightforward application of basic First Amendment principles: "When Government seeks to use its full power . . . to command where a person may get his or her information or what distrusted source he or she may not hear, it uses censorship to control thought. This is unlawful. The First Amendment confirms the freedom to think for ourselves."

Despite this logic, the campaign-finance clique has denounced the ruling as "judicial activism" and claimed that it contradicts a century of laws banning corporate money in elections. But this view of history is simply wrong. Although corporations have been prohibited from giving money directly to candidates since 1907, bans on independent corporate spending in elections did not go before the U.S. Supreme Court until 1990 in *Austin v. Michigan Chamber of Commerce*—a mere 20 years ago. The Court upheld the prohibition by a narrow 5–4 vote, but Austin was hardly a bedrock of constitutional law—indeed, it was the first case in Supreme

Court history to uphold a limit on independent political speech, which the Court in *Citizens United* correctly recognized as "a significant departure from ancient First Amendment principles." By reversing Austin, the Court has now corrected its error and brought the regulation of corporate and union speech in line with the rest of First Amendment doctrine.

When you hear reformers howl about the downfall of elections as a result of this ruling, consider that states [such as] Missouri, Utah, and Virginia already allow corporations to spend unlimited amounts on political ads, and there's no evidence that these states' elections have been "corrupted" or "overwhelmed" by this additional political speech. And that is not surprising. After all, no matter how much money is spent to promote or oppose candidates, voters remain free to disagree with those views. And they often do, as well-financed but failed candidates Ross Perot, Steve Forbes, Mitt Romney, and, more recently, Jon Corzine can attest.

But the reformers are not content to leave something as important as election results to voter free will. Their real complaint is not with the Supreme Court or its ruling in *Citizens United*, but with the First Amendment itself, which prohibits their efforts to empower government to micromanage political debate. The Founders saw the folly of that approach and gave us a First Amendment that rejected it in clear terms: "Congress shall make no law . . . abridging the freedom of speech." Despite the reformers' complaints, the ruling in *Citizens United* is faithful to the First Amendment, and that, ultimately, is the only test that matters.

11

The Supreme Court's Campaign Finance Decision Is Bad for Democracy

Richard L. Hasen

Richard L. Hasen is the William H. Hannon distinguished professor at Loyola Law School.

The Supreme Court, in its decision in Citizens United v. FEC, *has set back campaign finance reform. The ruling struck down federal campaign finance law restricting corporate spending in campaigns and also reversed a previous ruling. The court could have ruled narrowly on this case, but instead it made a broad ruling that sides with corporations. The court's decision opens the door for increased corruption and unchecked campaign spending.*

It is time for everyone to drop all the talk about the Roberts court's "judicial minimalism," with Chief Justice [John] Roberts as an "umpire" who just calls balls and strikes. Make no mistake, this is an activist court that is well on its way to recrafting constitutional law in its image. The best example of that is this morning's transformative opinion in *Citizens United v. FEC*. Today [January 21, 2010] the court struck down decades-old limits on corporate and union spending in elections (including judicial elections) and opened up our political system to a money free-for-all.

Back in June [2009], I explained to *Slate* readers the basics of this case. Citizens United is an ideological group, like the

NRA [National Rifle Association] or Planned Parenthood, except that it takes for-profit corporate funding. It produced an anti-Hillary Clinton documentary. The group wanted to air the documentary during the 2008 presidential primary season through a cable television video-on-demand service and to advertise for it on television. In exchange for a $1.2 million fee, a cable-television-operator consortium would have made the documentary available to subscribers to download free on demand. The McCain-Feingold campaign-finance law passed in 2002 bars certain corporate-funded television broadcasts, such as this documentary, in the 60 days before a general election (or the 30 days before a primary). And the law requires disclosure by the funders of election-related broadcast advertising, such as these ads. Citizens United argued against the corporate-spending ban.

Citizens United's broadest argument was that the court should overrule its 1990 case *Austin v. Michigan Chamber of Commerce*, which upheld limits on corporate spending in candidate elections. Before argument, I expected the court to take a different course by deciding this case narrowly. The court could have done that by saying that McCain-Feingold's statutory rules barring corporate-funded television broadcasts don't apply to video-on-demand broadcasts. That would be in line with some of the past decisions of the Roberts court, when it had preferred to chip away at existing precedent rather than dramatically move the law rightward. But, as [*Slate* editor] Dahlia Lithwick explained, at oral argument the government's lawyer got into some trouble in suggesting that the government would have the constitutional power to ban corporate-published *books* just before the election. The exchange made it seem like the court could well be poised to overrule *Austin*.

All bets were off at the end of the last term, when the court announced the case would be rescheduled for a second round of oral argument last September specifically to reconsider the overruling of *Austin* case and a second case, *McConnell*. We've been waiting ever since.

Today Justice [Anthony] Kennedy wrote for a court majority of the five conservative justices. He effectively wiped out a key provision of Congress' 2002 campaign finance reform. He also did indeed strike down *Austin* and parts of *McConnell*. To Justice Kennedy, any limits on the independent spending of money in elections smack of government censorship. The limits Congress enacted in 2002 remind him of old English laws requiring licensing for speech. He talked about the byzantine sets of federal laws and regulations involved—genuinely confusing, it's true—and said that none of it was permissible under the First Amendment. He talked of the rise of the Internet and blogs and how the government could soon come in and start regulating political blogging if the court did not step in.

Though the decision deals with federal elections, expect state and local corporate and union spending limits to be challenged, and to fall, throughout the country. There are many responses to Justice Kennedy's reasoning. He wrongly assumes that corporations or unions can throw money at public officials without corrupting them. Could a candidate for judicial office, for example, be swayed to rule in favor of a contributor who donated $3 million to an independent campaign to get the candidate elected to the state supreme court? Justice Kennedy himself thought so in last year's *Caperton v. A.T. Massey Coal Co., Inc.* case. And yet he runs away from that decision in today's ruling. Justice Kennedy acknowledges that with the "soft money" limits on political parties still in place, third-party groups (which tend to run more negative and irresponsible ads) will increase in strength relative to political parties. And that possibility raises the real chance Congress will repeal the "soft-money" limits, thereby increasing the risks of *quid pro quo* [literally: "Something for Something"] corruption.

There's more to criticize in the opinion. Should the American people, through Congress, be able to decide that the vast economic inequality that comes with our wonderful capitalist system should not translate into vast political inequality? Justice Kennedy seems to believe that this would lead to the imminent decline of our democracy. Money is speech; speech may not be suppressed. But the last time I checked, the U.K. and Canada were vibrant, functioning democracies, despite the far more stringent limits they place on spending in their elections. Finally, Justice Kennedy's single horrible—his specter of blog censorship—sounds more like the rantings of a right-wing talk show host than the rational view of a justice with a sense of political realism.

This is a court that has taken a giant leap toward deregulation of the electoral process.

What is so striking today is how avoidable this political tsunami was. The court has long adhered to a doctrine of "constitutional avoidance," by which it avoids deciding tough constitutional questions when there is a plausible way to make a narrower ruling based on a plain old statute. . . .

What we have in *Citizens United* is anti-avoidance. Kennedy's majority had to go out and grab this one. Justice [John Paul] Stevens' dissent lists three ways the majority could have skirted the constitutional question. One of them would have been to say that McCain-Feingold does not apply to video-on-demand. This and the Stevens' other options are all plausible interpretations. . . . Instead, here the court went out of its way to overturn its own precedent, in violation of its usual rule of *stare decisis* [to follow the precedents established by previous decisions], which calls for respecting past rulings for the good of reliable law-making. And it did so violating its usual rule, which it cited even yesterday, that it does not generally reach issues not raised in the initial petition to the court.

In short, the court did not have to do what it did today. The chief justice issued a brief concurrence apparently solely to defend himself (and Justice [Samuel] Alito, who signed it) against charges of judicial activism. Roberts wrote that the alternative interpretations were not plausible, and that exceptions to *stare decisis* apply. Opponents of the decision today are likely to be unconvinced. This is a court that has taken a giant leap toward deregulation of the electoral process.

It left in place one requirement: that the corporate and union groups unleashing the attack ads have to disclose who they are (and for that, Kennedy had everyone's vote but Justice [Clarence] Thomas'.) But given the history of money and elections, why should we think that disclosure alone will be enough to deal with the problems of corruption and inequality that threaten our government? I have my doubts. But I'm sure this is a bad day for American democracy.

12

Congress Should Pass the Fair Elections Now Act

Nick Nyhart and David Donnelly

Nick Nyhart is the president and chief executive officer of Public Campaign, a nonprofit organization advocating the elimination of big money and special interests from election campaigns. David Donnelly is the national campaigns director of Public Campaign Action Fund, a nonprofit aimed at improving campaign finance laws.

Congressional elections are driven by money, much of which comes from wealthy donors who often live outside the districts or states that the member candidates represent. This system divorces candidates from their constituents and makes them vulnerable to special-interest groups. To rectify the situation, Congress should pass the Fair Elections Now Act, a bill that would permit senators and representatives to seek funds from their constituents and then receive matching money from public grants to run competitive and evenly matched campaigns. This measure would force officials to reconnect with the citizens they represent and will give those voters a greater influence in the outcomes of these elections.

The 2008 elections were the most expensive in history, costing a record $5.3 billion. Although the next election is twenty months away [from March 2009], the pressure to raise even more money for 2010 is already bearing down on in-

Nick Nyhart and David Donnelly, "Fair Elections Now!" *The Nation*, vol. 288, April 13, 2009, pp. 6–7. Copyright © 2009 by The Nation Magazine/The Nation Company, Inc. Reproduced by permission.

cumbents. The economic crisis demands immediate and effective Congressional action, yet at this critical moment our politicians are being distracted by the need to fill their campaign war chests. Vulnerable House [of Representative] freshmen have been told by their party's campaign leaders to put $1 million in the bank before their first year is done. That's $20,000 each week without letup.

> The [Fair Elections Now Act] would require Congressional candidates to seek support from constituents back home, not from those in Washington or in wealthy enclaves around the country.

Fortunately, there's an alternative. Illinois Democrat Dick Durbin, Senate assistant majority leader, and Pennsylvania Republican Arlen Specter are introducing the Fair Elections Now Act, a measure that would turn the campaign fundraising system upside down. Set to move forward in the House are Democratic Caucus chair John Larson of Connecticut and North Carolina Republican Walter Jones, the lead sponsors of the Senate bill's companion measure. With powerful backers from the majority party leading the fight, a friend in the White House [President Barack Obama] and an angry public demanding action, the moment is ripe for a major structural reform that changes whose voices are heard in Washington [D.C.].

Seeking Support from Constituents

Senator Durbin, known for his pragmatic progressivism, has termed the campaign finance system "unsustainable." As fundraising demands have steadily increased, lawmakers have spent more time dialing up well-heeled donors, the vast majority of whom live nowhere near the lawmakers' districts, and less time gaining in-depth understanding of leading issues, crafting effective legislation with their colleagues or listening to their constituents.

Under Fair Elections, the rules are reversed. The measure would require Congressional candidates to seek support from constituents back home, not from those in Washington or in wealthy enclaves around the country. Participants would prove their viability by gathering large numbers of local supporters, not a large amount of money from the political class. House candidates who raise 1,500 small contributions from people in their state would qualify for a grant large enough to run a competitive campaign. Senate candidates would qualify by raising a specific number of contributions, determined by a formula that takes into account the number of Congressional districts in their state. The more populous the state, the higher the initial grant. If candidates want additional funds to address independent expenditures against them or to keep pace with a well-financed opponent, they can continue to raise donations of $100 or less, which are matched four times over with public money, up to a ceiling.

The proposal—modeled on elements of successful systems in Arizona, Connecticut, Maine, North Carolina and elsewhere—has profound implications for political organizing. For voters of average means, the benefits are compelling. Their small check, whether it's $10, $25 or $50, would be essential to a candidate's success. No longer would they worry that their elected officials are indebted to deep-pocket funders with interests entirely separate from their own. Community leaders with strong grassroots support would become more important and would help redefine the pool of potential candidates. The bill would create tremendous incentives for lawmakers to maintain a dialogue with their constituents; it would encourage participation by new faces in the electoral process and give citizens the ability to hold lawmakers accountable, even in heavily gerrymandered [divided for particular electoral results] districts.

Fair Elections would be attractive to incumbents as well, in two ways. First, the Capitol Hill fundraising grind would be replaced by increased contact with constituents. Second, the questions about conflicts of interest that inevitably follow big-money fundraising would disappear.

Overcoming Special Interests

Supporters of Fair Elections will likely find a strong ally in the president. As a senator, Barack Obama was the first co-sponsor of the 2007 version of the Durbin-Specter bill. His extraordinary success in raising small donations during the 2008 campaign demonstrated the possibility of a fundraising system that puts regular people ahead of inside-the-Beltway special interests. Now, as he presses forward with an expansive agenda for change, he could well be a leading beneficiary of a policy that would undercut the moneyed opposition to many of his proposals while reenergizing grassroots organizing.

The most critical matter before Congress and the White House is the economy, but other pressing issues demand attention as well: healthcare, energy, the global climate crisis, tax policy and government spending decisions. Without exception, these are concerns over which longstanding vested interests stand to gain or lose hundreds of billions of dollars. As the Obama administration and Congressional leaders grapple to find a delicate balance between quick fixes and savvy long-term policies—with a dose of smart politics—campaign donors have a heavy thumb on the scale [they have disproportionate influence]. Over the past two decades the financial sector has invested more than $5 billion in lobbying and campaign contributions to both parties, paying out the largest amount ever in the 2008 cycle. Energy interests and the medical industries have not been far behind, spending $455 million and $784 million, respectively, advancing their bottom-line interests over the same period.

The fierce policy battles ahead in Congress will draw clear lines between the narrow concerns of big contributors opposed to change and [the] policy solutions that serve the broad public interest. The Fair Elections bill, a bold initiative for ordinary citizens, offers a way out for lawmakers who for too long have been caught between the campaign money chase and the desire to serve their constituents. More important, it will increase voters' say over decisions that will have enormous consequences for their lives and for generations to come. In a democracy, we should demand no less.

13

The Fair Elections Now Act Is Impractical

Sean Parnell

Sean Parnell is the president of the Center for Competitive Politics, a First Amendment advocacy organization. He has written articles on campaign finance and other free speech issues for the New York Times, *the* Wall Street Journal, *and the* Washington Post.

The Fair Elections Now Act promises that by providing candidates with public funds to run campaigns, new voices and relative outsiders will be able to crack the network of established politicians and potentially gain public office. Unfortunately, if New York city's elections are any measure of using public funds to back candidates, the millions of taxpayer dollars spent ushered only one political outsider into office. Such schemes typically fail because many incumbents are self-financed and can spend their vast fortunes to defeat contenders. In addition, the network is so strong that most candidates for office are political insiders who have worked for years in government; few new candidates can acquire the campaign machinery or voter familiarity that these entrenched politicians already have working for them. Thus, spending public funds on races that are nearly always predetermined does not seem to be worthwhile reform.

A few weeks ago [in April 2009] Senators Dick Durbin (D-IL) and Arlen Specter (R-PA) introduced the "Fair Elections Now Act," the most recent version of so-called campaign

Sean Parnell, "What Will $24 Million in New York City's Taxpayer-Financed Campaigns Get You?" Center for Competitive Politics, April 21, 2009. Reproduced by permission.

finance "reform" to challenge the First Amendment (trying to roll over the First Amendment is nothing new for Senator Specter, who in the Fall of 2007 introduced a bill to change the First Amendment to exclude campaign contributions from its protection).

Although the new euphemism is apparently "fair elections," this is basically the same ... "clean elections" scheme that "reformers" have been pushing around the country for the past several years, handing out taxpayer dollars to politicians to pay for their campaigns instead of relying on the private, voluntary contributions of citizens.

Handing out Taxpayer Money to Candidates

In the course of researching and analyzing the Fair Elections Now Act proposal, I've been reading up on New York City's taxpayer-financed campaigns program, which has some similar aspects to the Fair Elections Now Act. Specifically, New York City will match the first $175 of any contribution made to a participating candidate, provided the donor lives in the city limits or, for city council races, in the district.

There's a tremendous amount of information available on New York City's program, much of it helpfully provided by the city's Campaign Finance Board in ... official reports. For example, the report on New York City's 2005 election reveals that the approximately $24 million in taxpayer money was distributed to candidates. So what did that $24 million buy?

Out of 51 city council races, only 7 featured open seats. All but one incumbent won re-election, most of them by significant margins (many of them didn't even face opponents). And the incumbent [who] lost? He was beaten after allegations of harassment and discrimination by his staffers, which netted him a $5,000 fine from the City Council, along with penalties imposed by the Campaign Finance Board. Needless to say, he did not have the best press during the election.

Oh, and the candidate who beat him? A former incumbent, who had been term-limited out after 2001.

There's absolutely no sign of outsiders or the ever-vaunted "average citizen" challenging the political establishment thanks to the help of New York's system of taxpayer subsidies for politicians.

Outsiders Rarely Beat Insiders

Of the 7 open seat races, 3 were won by obvious political insiders: 2 had served as chief of staff for the previous incumbent or Council speaker, and one was a district party leader and the daughter of a former State Assembly member. The other 4 also appeared to have strong ties to the political establishment—one was an employee of the powerful Service Employees union, who helped significantly in her campaign; another was district manager for the Bronx Community Board, apparently a local government unit in New York City; the third was a leading public figure on civil rights issues and an attorney with 2 Ivy League universities on his resume; and the fourth is described as a "community activist."

Of these 4 with less-obvious political ties, only the final candidate, community activist Darlene Mealy, could even possibly be described as a political outsider, someone who might possibly have had trouble raising funds without a matching program (although her endorsement by the *New York Times* and a variety of unions presumably would have gotten her over this barrier).

As for the other citywide races in the program, there's absolutely no sign of outsiders or the ever-vaunted "average citizen" challenging the political establishment thanks to the help of New York's system of taxpayer subsidies for politicians. Mayor Michael Bloomberg spent $84.6 million of his own money in his winning re-election campaign, incumbents won the Public Advocate and Comptroller positions (each getting 90 percent or more of the vote), and 4 of 5 Borough Presidents were easily re-elected. The Manhattan seat was open and was won by a sitting member of the New York State Assembly.

These numbers are important because schemes like the Fair Elections Now Act promise that "average citizens" will be able to run for office and win. One of the goals of the Fair Elections Now Act is, in fact, to "[create] genuine opportunities for all Americans to run for [Congress] and [encourage] more competitive elections." Apparently, it hasn't quite worked out that way in New York City.

So, $24 million in taxpayer funds shoveled into campaign coffers in New York City will, apparently, buy you (at best) one City Council seat filled by a candidate [who] *might* not have otherwise been able to raise enough money to mount a credible campaign. Maybe.

And the "reformers" wonder why we're skeptical of these schemes . . . .

14

Campaign Finance Reform Hurts Republicans

Gary Andres

Gary Andres is vice chairman of public policy and research at Dutko Worldwide, a bipartisan public policy advocacy organization. He has published articles in several major periodicals and writes a syndicated weekly column for the Weekly Standard Online.

Traditionally, the Republican Party has funded candidates with money that comes from political action groups and wealthy donors who support conservative ideals. When the Bipartisan Campaign Reform Act of 2002 restricted the amount of donations that either party could receive from these sources, the Republicans suffered greatly. Unlike the Democrats—who tend to gather contributions from a wide base of groups that support various liberal causes such as labor unions and environmental protection—the Republicans lack a host of issue-centered allies. When their main source of funds was curtailed, the Republicans could not look to outside organizations for help the way the Democrats could. Obviously, then, the Bipartisan Campaign Reform Act is biased legislation, giving a fundraising advantage to the Democrats, and because Democrats control Congress and the presidency following the 2008 election, it is unlikely that this unjust act will be overturned anytime soon.

Gary Andres, "Shortchanged: Why Campaign-Finance Reforms Hurt Republicans," *Weekly Standard*, April 23, 2009. Copyright © 2009 News America Inc., Weekly Standard. All rights reserved. Reproduced by permission.

It's no surprise that "change-minded" Democrats are mute on the issue of transforming the so-called toxic effect of money in politics. Since Democrats now have an overall cash advantage, why alter the game?

No doubt, Barack Obama possessed the Midas touch when it came to fundraising in 2008. But other factors related to how campaign finance laws affect the two parties are also at work. Evidence suggests political reforms aimed at limiting the parties' ability to raise resources have a disproportionately negative impact on the GOP [Republican Party]. Consider some recent history. The campaign finance system in 2008 offered [Republican candidate] John McCain a Hobson's choice [an illusory choice]. He could reject public financing and spend most of his time trying to compete with the Democratic nominee's money-machine. Or, he could accept the $84 million in federal funds and get buried by the avalanche of Obama cash.

It's unlikely that more financial resources alone could have saved the Republican presidential nominee. But it would have closed the huge advertising gap McCain faced in the last month of the campaign. The ad-tracking firm CMAG found Obama outspent his Republican opponents four to one in the final weeks of the campaign, according to University of Massachusetts political science professor Raymond J. La Raja.

Republicans Supported Reform

Ironically, Republicans had a role in writing the very laws that put their nominee in this difficult position. Most opponents of the Bipartisan Campaign Reform Act (BCRA) passed in 2002 blame Republican sponsors such as McCain, who was indeed one of the co-authors of the legislation. But President George W. Bush also played a role in its enactment by signing the bill.

And the irony for Republicans continues. When Mr. McCain chose to accept the limited federal funds, he also had to rely on the Republican National Committee [RNC] to help fill the money gap. But national political committees were severely restricted in their money-raising abilities, by—you guessed it—the BCRA. Prior to enactment of the 2002 reforms, national political committees, like the RNC and DNC [Democratic National Committee], could raise large sums of money not regulated by the federal campaign finance laws because it was used for issue advertising (not specifically advocating the election or defeat of candidates), party-building, get-out-the-vote efforts, or administrative purposes. Because these funds were outside the scope of federal campaign limits on contributions, it was called "soft money." BCRA banned these contributions.

The dispersion of finances tends to benefit Democrats because their political culture includes more allied groups who benefit from a distributional big bang.

Professor La Raja agrees that both recent elections and history underscore a fundamental point about campaign finance reform: Changes aimed at restricting political parties usually hurt Republicans more than Democrats. In his new book *Small Change: Money, Political Parties and Campaign Finance Reform*, La Raja points to several historical examples where new anti-party regulations hamstrung the GOP.

This is because the more disparate Democratic party has always relied on a wider assortment of outside allies, according to La Raja. "Throughout much of the party's history, the Democrats never used the central organizing model of the Republicans because the party has always been a looser construction of political interests," he argues in the book. "Instead, allied interest groups—labor unions, environmental groups, African-American churches and community organizations—have engaged voter mobilization for party candidates. In contrast, the Republican Party lacks a natural, member-oriented organization that pulls in volunteers and mobilizes voters. Beyond the Christian Right, whose enthusiasm varies depending on the candidate's affinity for their goals, the Republican Party must rely on the party infrastructure."

In other words, reforms aimed at political parties don't limit money but rather scatter it throughout the system. And due to the differences between the two political parties in America, the dispersion of finances tends to benefit Democrats because their political culture includes more allied groups who benefit from a distributional big bang.

More Shadow Funds, Less Transparency

Not long after last November's [2008] election, the RNC sought to overturn portions of the BCRA restrictions on soft-dollar contributions. It's unclear whether these efforts will succeed. If they don't, Republicans will have to encourage the formation of alliances with non-party, allied groups—like the Democrats do—to help fill the financial hole. It won't be easy, and it won't be pretty. It will also likely move more money, power, and influence back into the unreported shadows. At least major political committees like the RNC and DNC have some public accountability because of their close links to elected officials. Under today's new collection of [so-called] 527 organizations and 501 (c) groups [both non-profit], it's like we've entered a new Wild West period of politics in America.

But don't look to the Obama administration or Democrats in Congress to help topple the current system. The "reforms" imposed by the BCRA did the same thing that previous changes in the campaign finance laws have done—stack the deck against the GOP.

15

America Needs a Small-Donor, Public-Funded Campaign Finance System

Mark Schmitt

Mark Schmitt is the executive editor of The American Prospect. *Previously he was a senior fellow at the New America Foundation, director of the Governance and Public Policy program at the Open Society Institute, and policy director to Senator Bill Bradley.*

The 2008 presidential race proved that small-donor contributions could fund a successful campaign because a high percentage of the populace was motivated to raise funds and vote. It is still important to restrict large contributions and expand on the model of small-donor participant democracy, however. To this end, lawmakers should consider providing public matching funds for small donations and giving tax credits for such contributions. If small donors are given incentives to participate in campaigns and empowered to band together, they may indeed offset the power of big-money interests and ensure that future elections are driven by the will of the people.

Early last year, as the 2008 presidential campaign loomed on the horizon, campaign-finance experts and newspaper editorial boards warned preemptively of a "billion-dollar election." In a February 2007 editorial, *The New York Times* in-

Mark Schmitt, "Can Money Be a Force for Good?" *The American Prospect*, vol. 20, January–February 2009, pp. A13–A15. Copyright © 2009 The American Prospect, Inc. All rights reserved. Reproduced with permission from The American Prospect, 11 Beacon Street, Suite 1120, Boston, MA 02108.

voked Watergate [a scandal involving burglary and wiretapping of the Democratic National Committee that President Richard Nixon attempted to cover up] to warn that such an expensive election would represent a breakdown of campaign-finance regulation and mark a return to the corruption of the Nixon era. If [Democratic candidate] Senator Hillary Clinton were looking for a clever name for her big fundraisers, something comparable to George W. Bush's "Pioneers," she could, the editorial suggested, call them "Recidivists." (After marveling at the millions that Clinton, Rudy Giuliani, and a few other candidates had already amassed, news stories at the time mentioned in passing that there was also a fellow named Barack Obama [another Democratic candidate] who had raised $500,000.)

In the end, more than $1.6 billion was raised for the presidency alone, more than twice as much as was raised four years earlier. A single candidate—Barack Obama—raised and spent $640 million of that total. Candidates for the House [of Representatives] and Senate spent more than a billion dollars, even though, as always, most contests were not competitive. All told, the predicted billion-dollar election actually cost $5.3 billion, according to the Center for Responsive Politics.

A Small-Donor Success Story

Only a few presidential candidates participated in the public-financing system for the primaries. One, Obama, was the first candidate since the system was created to opt out of using it in the general election, passing up $85 million in no-strings-attached money in favor of continuing to raise hundreds of millions in private donations. Meanwhile, the other major-party candidate [John McCain] supplemented public financing with $19 million in coordinated funding through the Republican National Committee and at least $36 million through a legal loophole known as a General Election Legal and Accounting Compliance Fund.

Had these staggering circumstances been predicted to campaign-finance reform advocates a few years ago, they would have unanimously described them as a dystopia, a terrifying fate for American democracy and evidence of the collapse of not only the 2002 Bipartisan Campaign Reform Act (the McCain-Feingold law) but the entire edifice of post-Watergate election reforms.

More than 3 million donors gave to the Obama campaign alone.

Yet when that day came, many of the same reformers described it as one of the brighter days in the history of American democracy. Voters participated in record numbers, and enthusiasm was palpable, not just for Obama but for other presidential candidates as well as House and Senate candidates. Despite the record number of voters who told pollsters that the country was on the "wrong track" and the unprecedented disapproval ratings for both the president and Congress, there were strong signals that voters were motivated by hope. Unusually high percentages of people told the Pew poll that they were voting *for* their preferred candidate rather than *against* the other.

And while the amount of money was staggering, so was the number of people involved: More than 3 million donors gave to the Obama campaign alone. Though we don't have good historical data on donors who give less than $200 (the amount required to be reported), we know that in 1996, only 567,000 people gave $200 or more to *any* candidate or party, and only 200,000 people gave to any Democrat or the Democratic Party. By comparison, 322,000 donors gave $200 or more to Obama's campaign, in addition to the roughly 2.7 million who sent smaller amounts. More than 1.2 million people donated $200 or more to campaigns—not only Obama's—in 2008, according to the Center for Responsive

Politics. Such a broad and diverse base of donors and the astonishing percentage of small donors (48 percent of Obama's funds and 34 percent of John McCain's came from individuals who gave less than $200) have to significantly alleviate concerns about corruption resulting from the leverage that any individual donor, group of donors, or major fundraiser would hold. In this new world dominated by small donations, no one individual has much sway over the candidate.

Money, positive engagement with politics and government, and participation can, in certain circumstances, form a virtuous circle.

A Level of Public Support That Cannot Be Repeated

Two facts revealed by the 2008 election—the collapse of the campaign-finance regulatory regime and the transformation of small-donor fundraising—call for not just new rules but an entirely new set of assumptions about money in politics. Campaign-finance law treats money in isolation as a bad and corrupting force that should be constrained or eliminated. The authors of the existing laws assumed that small donors were unlikely to play a major part in politics unless constraints on large contributions and on soft-money contributions from corporations and unions forced candidates to go small. And they assumed that money, cynicism, and low participation formed a vicious circle.

These are the assumptions of 1996, when only half a million or so people were involved in politics as contributors and when political participation was at its lowest level ever. (That was the only year in American history when voter turnout fell below 50 percent.) We now know two things we didn't know then: Small donors *can* be drawn to politics, and large sums of money in politics and engaged, participatory democracy are not incompatible; money can, in fact, be an essential form of expression that deepens participation. That is, money, positive engagement with politics and government, and participation can, in certain circumstances, form a virtuous circle.

The election created a paradox: If there were a causal relationship between big money in politics and corruption, public cynicism, and low participation, then a year like 2008—which featured big money but also public enthusiasm and high participation—should not exist. Longtime opponents of reform, such as former Federal Election Commissioner Bradley Smith, jumped on the result as proof that they had been right all along: "Obama's fundraising shows us the emptiness of the arguments for campaign finance 'reform,'" Smith wrote in *The Washington Post* a week before Election Day.

Obama, who had earlier made a vague pledge to work out an agreement with his opponent whereby both would accept public financing, and was widely criticized for opting out, described his fundraising base as "a parallel public-financing system where the American people decide, if they want to support a campaign, they can get on the Internet and finance it."

He was right in one sense and wrong in another. It is fair to consider his 3 million donors "public financing." A broad base of support, reflecting such enthusiasm that roughly one out of every 30 people who voted for him also made a contribution, can legitimately be called public.

The Internet, in particular, made a new kind of small-donor fundraising possible.

What it cannot be called, however, is a "system." The circumstances that led to Obama's ability to raise almost twice as much money as any previous candidate are not reproducible. And some of the circumstances—such as the extraordinary polarization of the electorate and the passion for change after eight years of [President] George W. Bush—one would never want to reproduce. Certain congressional candidates, especially those who won attention among the online activists of the "netroots," also brought in astonishing levels of small donations. But for the most part there was no change in the price of a competitive congressional race or in the advantage held by incumbents and those with access to larger donors, according to an immediate post-election study by the Campaign Finance Institute.

The Role of Technology

Indeed, as 14 scholars agreed in the journal *The Forum*, published by the University of California, Berkeley, the regime by which we govern money in politics has "collapsed." The regulations intended to control large contributions and soft money, bolstered by the McCain-Feingold reforms of 2002, were weakened by the Federal Election Commission and finally made irrelevant last year by the Supreme Court's correct ruling that issue advertisements mentioning a candidate near election time cannot be regulated. The 34-year-old public-financing system, an outdated model whose flaws were evident, died from disuse.

While the constructed elements of the campaign-finance system—legal fundraising limits and formal public financing—collapsed, the system was saved by accidental developments outside of the legal framework. The Internet, in particular, made a new kind of small-donor fundraising possible. In the past, asking a donor for a second or third donation was costly, so all the incentives were to ask for a large donation up front. Beginning with [Democratic candidate] Howard Dean's campaign in 2004, campaigns understood that, with a donor's e-mail address in hand, asking for more money was cost-free. Now there was every reason to ask a donor for $5 or $10 to start with and nothing lost if the donor had only $5 or $10 to give. This is not some technological miracle but a small change with huge consequences made possible by technology.

Technology also slashed the transaction costs of organizing to raise money outside the campaigns or parties. A decade ago, the only interests that could organize to raise and contribute money collectively were those with the financial incentive that made it worth the huge costs of organizing to influence government—the large trade associations of Washington's K Street, for example, or a few organized groups of single-issue voters such as gun-rights supporters. Thus a primary goal of reform was to limit such organizations, whether in the form of political action committees (PACs) or the "527" [nonprofit] committees that emerged in 2004. [Because] the ability to organize was distributed unequally, regulating organizing was essential to equality.

Small-donor democracy is a change of orientation, so that instead of trying to purge politics of big money or organized money, we ensure that money can be a force for good.

But Internet intermediaries such as *ActBlue.com*, a clearinghouse for individuals or groups to raise money for candidates they favor, have completely transformed the nature of organizing. *ActBlue* users, acting independently, have raised $83 million for candidates since the site launched in 2004. This, in turn, enabled candidates to raise money without going through the gatekeepers of the big, organized dollars—the lobbyists and financiers—and changed the range of issues that candidates had to respond to. (While the most notable achievements of low-transaction-cost political organizing have been on the left, it is a matter of time before comparable conservative organizations such as *Slatecard.com* catch up.) Numerous congressional candidacies, such as that of newly elected Representative Tom Periello in Virginia, would never have been possible, much less victorious, without *ActBlue* and the thousands who use it to organize.

The challenge in the next wave of reform is not to try to rebuild the post-Watergate campaign-finance regulations but instead to see money as one factor in a larger system and intervene to turn money into a force for good (participation, robust communication) rather than for ill (corruption, massive inequality in the ability of candidates to be heard). Neither the laissez-faire view that opposes reform nor the traditional reform approach based on limiting contributions and closing loopholes recognizes these possibilities. The goal should be to understand the achievements of Obama, *ActBlue*, and others and institutionalize them into a real system that works for voters and all candidates.

Creating a System That Works

Such a system would seek to create every incentive for small donors to participate and for candidates and parties to seek small donors, especially in the early stages of a campaign. Small-donor democracy is not a single legislative fix. Rather, it is a change of orientation, so that instead of trying to purge politics of big money or organized money, we use the lessons of 2008 to ensure that money can be a force for good. There are a few key ways to fashion a small-donor democracy system that can work for all candidates:

- Change the incentives for candidates to seek small donations. A generous match on small contributions, such as New York City's 6-to-1 public match, is one way to give candidates as much motivation to seek a $50 contribution as a $300 contribution. Even systems of full public financing, such as Arizona's, use small contributions as seed money to prove broad public support. As that state's governor, Janet Napolitano, has said, it led her to approach the same people for money that she approaches for votes.

- Create new ways for small donors to give. Legal scholar Bruce Ackerman has long advocated a system of "patriot dollars"—a voucher given to every citizen to contribute to a candidate or a political organization. The same goals can be achieved through a refundable tax credit for small contributions, especially if it were well publicized. Minnesota's system combines a matching system with a tax credit, appealing to both candidates and contributors.

- Add new incentives for small-dollar organizing. To offset the power of big political organizations, add new incentives for small-donor PACs, such as those organized on *ActBlue*, by making contributions to certain qualified political organizations eligible for the match or tax credit as well.

These provisions could be combined in various ways so that a public-financing system could have both a matching system for candidates to get started and then full public financing once a certain level of support were reached. Such systems would be flexible, not locking candidates into spending limits or other restrictions that limit their ability to respond if outspent, the core problem of the old presidential system. They respect the role of money as a legitimate expression of enthusiasm and a form of participation. And they build on healthy trends in our politics rather than continuing the futile quest to build a wall against unhealthy trends.

16

The Internet Will Shape the Future of Campaign Finance

James A. Barnes

James A. Barnes is the political correspondent for National Journal *and creator of the* National Journal Insiders Poll, *which gauges expert opinion on various political issues.*

Although presidential candidates have taken advantage of Internet fundraising since 2000, Barack Obama, the Democratic contender in the 2008 race, received recognition for the sheer amounts of financing he raised via small-donor, electronic contributions. Candidates such as Obama have learned to use Internet meet-up sites and search engine advertising to rake in donations while also gauging public interest in specific issues. Because of Obama's success, future candidates will probably have to master Internet fundraising in order to compete with their opponents.

It was an unusual time for a presidential candidate to extol the value of his small donors, but that didn't deter Barack Obama. The Democratic front-runner told a roomful of supporters who had forked over $1,000 to $2,300 apiece to attend the April 8 [2008] fundraiser, "We have created a parallel public financing system where the American people decide if they want to support a campaign, [and then] they can get on the Internet and finance it. And they will have as much access and influence over the course and direction of our campaign [as] has traditionally [been] reserved for the wealthy and the powerful."

James A. Barnes, "Online Fundraising Revolution," *National Journal*, vol. 40, April 19, 2008, pp. 36–38. Copyright 2009 by National Journal Group Inc. Reproduced by permission.

To be sure, Obama's prodigious fundraising machine has collected more than its share of large checks from the "wealthy and the powerful," including $500,000 worth at the Washington [D.C.] event where he rhapsodized about the supporters who click in with more-modest contributions. And Obama's advisers hastened to add that his comments were not a signal that he would opt out of the 32-year-old public financing system for the general election, something that no presidential nominee—Democrat or Republican—has ever done.

The generally accepted definition of a "small donor" is someone who contributes less than $200. Through February [2008], about 90 percent of Obama's donors fit that description.

But the senator's remarks underscored an amazing point: He probably could. In the past, a candidate who was spending $1 million a day in a fierce struggle for his party's presidential nomination would hardly be in a position to consider turning down an $84 million check from Uncle Sam to fund a nine-and-a-half-week-long campaign in the fall. Then again, no other candidate has ever built such an enormous fundraising base.

Small Donors Fueled Obama's Campaign Machine

Well over a million people donated more than $230 million to Obama's campaign through the first quarter of this year [2008]. And, fueled by his Internet fundraising machine of small donors, the candidate pulled in more than 40 percent of that cash in just two months, $55 million in February and $40 million in March. During that brief time, Obama almost doubled his donor pool to 1.3 million, his campaign says. Obama hopes to have 1.5 million donors by early May.

In political circles, the generally accepted definition of a "small donor" is someone who contributes less than $200. Through February [2008], about 90 percent of Obama's donors fit that description, according to information from his campaign and the nonpartisan Center for Responsive Politics. If March continued that trend, Obama has more than 1.1 million small donors.

Even if that estimate is a bit high, Obama's army of small donors is nevertheless very impressive. According to an analysis by the Campaign Finance Institute and the Institute for Politics, Democracy & the Internet, a total of 625,000 small donors gave money to a major-party presidential candidate in 2000. In the 2004 race, that number surged to between 2 million and 2.8 million. Obama is already halfway to that historic high—with six more months to add donors to his fold if he wins the Democratic nomination and opts out of public financing.

A Unique Time in Election History

The significance of Obama's record-shattering success as a fundraiser is enormous. His donor base puts him in a position to become the first insurgent candidate to win a major party's presidential nomination since 1976, when Jimmy Carter won the Democratic nod in the first election under the public financing regime. Obama's financial advantage over Democratic rival Hillary Rodham Clinton enabled him to outspend her in the string of post-Super Tuesday contests in which he built his lead in pledged delegates and established himself as his party's clear front-runner.

Political analysts have traditionally viewed public financing as the ally of insurgents because the system offers a federal match for individual contributions of up to $250 once a candidate agrees to abide by certain restrictions. The system can give little-known candidates the ability to raise enough money to compete in the early primaries and caucuses against establishment candidates with national fundraising bases. The regime also puts caps on the amount of money that candidates can spend in individual states and in the overall campaign—limits that can help level the financial playing field. (In the current campaign cycle, all of the remaining candidates declined to participate in the public financing system for the primary season.)

Some political observers and scholars, however, suspect that the caps actually disadvantage insurgents by preventing them from raising enough money to overcome establishment candidates' inherent advantages, such as endorsements and support from party leaders, elected officials, and interest groups.

Obama isn't the first contender to strike political gold on the Internet.

To be sure, the grassroots energy behind Obama's candidacy is a vital ingredient in his success, but having the dollars to build an organizational apparatus to harness that excitement has also been key. "There's no question his fundraising capacity has been a big factor for him in some of these states," said veteran Democratic presidential strategist Tad Devine.

So, is Internet fundraising likely to transform the next presidential contest and other races? "I think that we all are sort of learning some tactics and principles, ideas, and tools that will apply in the future," said a Democratic consultant and senior Obama strategist who requested anonymity. "But I do think there is a foundation of uniqueness that drives this stuff for this campaign that is uncommon in campaigns."

Past Successes and New Record Hauls

Obama isn't the first contender to strike political gold on the Internet. In 2000, it was Republican John McCain who became the first presidential candidate to benefit from Internet fundraising. In the week after the senator from Arizona won the New Hampshire primary that year, supporters flooded his campaign website with $2.2 million in contributions.

"It was all over-the-transom money," recalls Becki Donatelli, chairman of Campaign Solutions, an Internet fundraising consulting firm that counts McCain as a client. "There is still that today, but it's also become part of Fundraising 101 [to include online] direct marketing in addition to creating a [website] where people bubble up."

In the 2004 Democratic presidential nominating contest, former Vermont Governor Howard Dean was the Internet's darling. In the year leading up to the primaries, Dean collected more than twice as much money as his nearest rival on the fundraising front, Senator John Kerry of Massachusetts.

Dean's campaign used the popular Internet social-networking site *Meetup.com* to gather and galvanize supporters. The campaign also created an interactive baseball bat on its own website to periodically challenge supporters to send in contributions for a particular cause or by a certain time. As contributions rolled, in, the virtual bat would fill up like mercury rising in a thermometer.

In one novel challenge, Dean successfully exhorted his donors to contribute $250,000 in a single day to offset the sum that Vice President [Dick] Cheney planned to raise at a luncheon with GOP [Grand Old Party, that is, the Republican Party] fat cats. "What drove all of this was the enthusiasm that people had for Howard Dean. The Internet is a bunch of wires. If you have the juice, things will move," said veteran Democratic direct-mail fundraiser Hal Malchow. Internet fundraising can often resemble "donors chasing fundraisers," he joked. "It's kind of an unnatural act."

Internet fundraising tends to track the emotional highs and lows of a political contest, but sometimes in unexpected ways. Two days after Obama lost the New Hampshire primary to Clinton, he raised twice the amount that McCain had raised in the week after his 2000 victory in the Granite State—some $4.4 million. Clinton has had good money-raising streaks, too. In the two days after her strong showing in Ohio and Texas on March 4 [2008], she took in about $4 million.

Obama's record $55 million haul in February—$45 million of which was contributed online—was boosted by his early victories. "There was that enthusiasm and excitement to giving: 'Obama won another election,'" an Obama strategist said. "That's one of the reasons why February was so extraordinary."

Still, even an also-ran presidential candidate who barely drew any actual votes broke online fundraising records earlier this year. Rep. Ron Paul, R-Texas, raked in more than $4.2 million in a single day when a Florida music promoter linked an Internet appeal for the anti-war libertarian to Guy Fawkes Day, the November 5 anniversary of the attempt to blow up the British Parliament in 1605. Paul's campaign went on to raise some $6.2 million over the Internet on December 16, the anniversary of the Boston Tea Party.

But Obama is the clear leader in taking Internet fundraising to new heights. In the spring and summer of 2007, the Obama campaign held rallies that drew 5,000 people, 10,000 people, or more. Partly to manage such large crowds, the campaign had asked supporters to sign up online or at campaign offices in advance to attend a rally. That sign-up process yielded a lot of e-mail addresses. At the same time, the Obama campaign was beginning to build its online community, giving supporters opportunities to meet one another and volunteer for door-to-door canvassing, phone-banking, and other activities.

Search Engine Advertising

The presidential campaigns have recently adopted an online fundraising tool linked to search engines. And once again, the Obama campaign has shown the way.

On Google, the Web's most popular search engine, the company's advertising program, AdWords, allows a campaign (or any other advertiser) to sponsor an ad that pops up next to the results page when a user's search includes particular key words. The campaign pays Google only when someone actually clicks on its ad. If the campaign buys more than one triggering word—"Iraq" and "immigration," say—the advertising program indicates which word lured the new supporter to its ranks. That information can help the campaign tailor messages to particular subsets of Obama boosters.

In the world of politics, presidential campaigns are today's biggest users of search engine advertising to reach out to potential donors instead of waiting for them to find the candidate's website. But down-ballot campaigns [those of political contenders whose contests are voted on alongside presidential ones] are increasingly joining in. "I think there will be a day pretty soon where everyone from presidential to state legislative candidates will be using Google AdWords and other tools," predicts Peter Greenberger, team manager for Google's Elections & Issue Advocacy business unit.

Social trends are likely to make that happen. Direct mail, the traditional mainstay for attracting small donors, has been most effective among the oldest voters. "As long as we have a constituency who doesn't do [electronic] commerce—meaning, use their credit card to make a purchase or give a donation—direct mail will be alive," said one 2008 presidential Internet strategist. "But as they die, so will direct mail."

Raising money over the phone, another staple of campaigns past, has grown more difficult as people have given up land lines and rebelled against telemarketers. "The future for the telemarketing industry in politics is not especially bright as more and more state legislatures look for more-robust enforcement of Do Not Call lists," said Philip Musser, president of New Frontier Strategy, a public-relations firm that focuses on state issues. Musser, who also advises Google on politics and state issues, noted that the Internet allows people to "consume [a fundraising appeal] at their pleasure rather than be forced to hear a message when they don't want to."

Future Candidates Are Likely to Use the Internet for Fundraising

Whether future presidential candidates will replicate Obama's Internet fundraising machine remains to be seen, but White House hopefuls of both parties are sure to try. Given the range of candidates who have succeeded to some extent at "Net-raising," from McCain to Dean to Clinton to Paul, tomorrow's contenders will probably expect to be able to light up the Net-roots.

Moreover, if Obama is the eventual Democratic nominee, political elites and the news media will surely expect future candidates to demonstrate the ability to raise money on the Internet just as they now must show that they can sign up impressive names for their finance committees.

If a candidate can't milk the Internet like a cash cow, said University of Wisconsin political scientist Byron Shafer, an authority on the presidential nominating process, "then we know you'll be limited to what the bundlers can drag out for you. You're not going to start a campaign and say, 'This wild Obama thing, I'm not going to bother.' You're going to hire a guy and say, 'Make this work for me.'"

17

Despite Reform Measures, Money Will Always Influence Politics

P.J. O'Rourke

P.J. O'Rourke is a political satirist and columnist for The Atlantic *and a frequent contributor to* The Weekly Standard *and* The American Spectator. *He is also the author of many books, including* Eat the Rich *and* Peace Kills: America's Fun New Imperialism.

Campaign finance rules are a confusing mess, leaving loopholes large enough for outlawed "soft-money" contributors to find ways to fund candidates. Furthermore, though the candidates have often tried to remain above the influence of money, they nonetheless accept whatever comes into their coffers when running expensive campaigns. Regardless of the moral rectitude of contenders or the restrictions enacted by disenchanted reformers, money will always find a way into the U.S. election process.

We have held our first cleaned-up national elections [in 2004] under the McCain-Feingold Bipartisan Campaign Reform Act of 2002. The act banned "soft money"—money previously exempt from federal campaign—contribution limits. Individuals and organizations can no longer make unlimited donations to political parties for "party-building activities." Such activities might have included producing vituperative TV ads calling a decorated-war-hero senator a

P.J. O'Rourke, "Incumbent-Protection Acts," *The Atlantic*, vol. 295, April 2005, p. 36. Copyright 2005 The Atlantic Media Co., as first published in The Atlantic Magazine. Distributed by Tribune Media Services. Reproduced by permission.

goldbrick, or sponsoring hysterical Web sites accusing the president's father of being King Faisal's fifth wife.

Under our freshly purified electoral system, individuals and organizations had to do that themselves. They used "527" committees, named after a section of the U.S. tax code that allows tax-free political advocacy as long as it doesn't go too far and, well, advocate a politician. One suspects that some of the 527s were cheating.

This will be fixed soon. The usual suspects behind campaign reform have introduced legislation to eliminate the 527 version of soft money. Two congressmen have sued the Federal Election Commission [FEC] for failing to regulate 527s. And the FEC itself has imposed restrictions on 527s beginning this year [2005].

An extra billion in campaign funds raised despite onerous new restrictions is an example of the ingenuity and flexibility that make our democracy successful, even if it is corrupted by money.

More Money, More Corruption

Further laws and lawsuits will be needed to regulate the political advocacy of slovenly, loudmouthed leftist filmmakers, wild-eyed evangelicals raving from pulpits, and you and me. Politics must be freed from the corruption of money.

We have a ways to go. Last year, for the first time, victorious campaigns for the House [of Representative] cost an average of more than $1 million. Outlays for victorious Senate campaigns rose by 47 percent. Total spending on presidential, Senate, and House races was almost $4 billion, versus approximately $3 billion in 2000, before McCain-Feingold.

Thus McCain-Feingold has not been a success. Unless it has. Americans are 33 percent more politically involved than they were four years ago, if we measure involvement in dollars. And an extra billion in campaign funds raised despite onerous new restrictions is an example of the ingenuity and flexibility that make our democracy successful, even if it is corrupted by money.

Do the possessors of money wield too much influence? They do at the mall, doubtless likewise in politics.

The word "corruption" comes from the Latin *rumpere*, "to break." Anyone who has experienced the politics of a volunteer board, a social club, or a college English department knows that politics is cracked and fractured, money be damned. Humbugs and Hitlers say politics makes people whole.

Is there too much money in politics? There are some 209 million Americans of voting age. The 2004 presidential campaigns spent about $1.2 billion. Would you sell your vote for $5.74? (Well, last year, yes—if it would have made the candidates go away.)

Do the possessors of money wield too much influence? They do at the mall, doubtless likewise in politics. Yet telecommunications companies, some of America's richest corporations, are pestered by the government while agriculture—making up less than 1.5 percent of GDP [gross domestic product]—is amply subsidized.

Furor over Fundraising

It would take a Bill Clinton's worth of political knowledge to understand how this policy results from campaign corruption. Interestingly, it's a holdover Clinton appointee, Bradley A. Smith, who is the nation's most eloquent critic of campaign reform. More interestingly, Smith is a member of the Federal Election Commission. He believes that all restrictions on campaign giving and spending are violations of the First Amendment. Not a mere free-speech nut, Smith also believes that spending restrictions give too much power to the media. Smith called the Federal Election Campaign Act of 1971 an "Incumbent Protection Act," because it limited big-giver seed money for unknown candidates. (In Washington they say that to run for office you need "a Rolex or a Rolodex.") Smith is even dubious about the disclosure of campaign contributions. He cites the 1958 Supreme Court ruling, in *NAACP v. Alabama*, that the anonymity of donors to a cause is protected by the First Amendment. Bradley Smith thinks we should ignore who gives what to whom and judge candidates by their ideals, ideas, and actions.

If that would help. The perpetuation of slavery, the exile and extermination of American Indians, and the passage of Jim Crow [segregation] laws weren't carried out at the bidding of a few malefactors of great wealth. These policies had support among ordinary voters—the individual small-donor types that McCain-Feingold is supposed to encourage. And indeed, the number of individual donors to the populist Democratic Party rose nearly sevenfold in the 2004 election cycle. Of course, Democrats are all good, progressive people nowadays. So we should just restrict campaign contributions from bad, regressive special interests.

We've been trying since 1757, when George Washington, running for the Virginia House of Burgesses, was criticized for serving a quart and a half of liquor to each voter. Under progressive Democratic administrations campaign-finance-reform acts were passed in 1939, 1943, 1947, and 1967. But wait. Under selfish, special-interest-dominated Republican administrations campaign-finance-reform acts were passed in 1883, 1907, 1910, 1911, 1925, 1971, 1974, and 2009. No less a mossback [an old-fashioned conservative] than Barry Goldwater once co-sponsored a bill to cap donations by political-action committees.

Neither liberal nor conservative politicians can resist the temptation to stand as mighty sequoias of rectitude amid the lowly underbrush of fundraising. But, says the political strategist Ralph Reed, "money is like water down the side of the mountain. It will find a way to get around the trees."

Organizations to Contact

The editors have compiled the following list of organizations concerned with the issues debated in this book. The descriptions are derived from materials provided by the organizations. All have publications or information available for interested readers. The list was compiled on the date of publication of the present volume; the information provided here may change. Be aware that many organizations take several weeks or longer to respond to inquiries, so allow as much time as possible.

American Enterprise Institute (AEI)
1150 Seventeenth Street NW, Washington, DC 20036
(202) 862-5800 • fax: (202) 862-7177
Web site: www.aei.org

The nonpartisan, public policy organization AEI strives to promote the ideals of free enterprise, individual opportunity, and a strong national defense through its conferences, publication of newsletters and books, and encouragement of open debate. Within the institute's politics and elections research area, analysts suggest opportunities for reforming both political institutions and campaign finance. Reports and commentary outlining these suggestions can be found on the AEI Web site along with a link to the journal of the institute, *The American*. The AEI Press also published the book *Better Parties, Better Government: A Realistic Program for Campaign Finance Reform* by Peter J. Wallison and Joel M. Gora in April 2009.

Brennan Center for Justice
161 Avenue of the Americas, 12th Floor, New York, NY 10013
(212) 998-6730 • fax: (212) 995-4550
E-mail: brennancenter@nyu.edu
Web site: www.brennancenter.org

The Brennan Center for Justice, a nonpartisan public policy and law institute, works as a think tank, public interest law firm, and advocacy group to effect positive change in the public sector. The center advocates for campaign finance reform that requires disclosure of the sources of potentially influential campaign contributions, contribution limitations to reduce the influence of money on politicians, and the retention of public funding to ensure the continued influence of voters and competitive elections. The Brennan Center has published a number of reports on campaign finance reform, all available on its Web site, such as "Money in Politics 2009: New Horizons for Reform," "Electoral Competition and Low Contribution Limits," and "Writing Reform: A Guide to Drafting State & Local Campaign Finance Laws."

Brookings Institution
1775 Massachusetts Ave. NW, Washington, DC   20036
(202) 797-6000
Web site: www.brookings.edu

The Brookings Institution, a nonprofit public policy organization, seeks to strengthen the American democratic system; improve economic and social wellbeing, security, and opportunity for all American citizens; and establish international security, prosperity, and cooperation. With regard to campaign finance reform, the institute has conducted extensive research to assess whether recent reforms have actually helped to limit the influence of money on American elections. Reports such as "A Collapse of the Campaign Finance Regime?" "A Report on the 2008 Presidential Nomination Ads," and "Campaign Finance Reform: Are There Smarter Ways to Fix the System?" can be found on the Brookings Web site.

Campaign Finance Information Center (CFIC)
C/O Investigative Reporters and Editors, 138 Neff Annex
Missouri School of Journalism, Columbia, MO   65211
(573) 882-2042 • fax: (573) 882-5431
E-mail: cfic-comments@ire.org
Web site: www.campaignfinance.org

CFIC is based at the Missouri School of Journalism and has as its mission aiding journalists in investigating and reporting the financial aspects of national, state, and local elections. The

CFIC Web site provides state-by-state campaign finance information as well as links to additional articles and Web sites detailing financial contributions to elections nationwide.

Campaign Finance Institute (CFI)

1667 K Street NW, Suite 650, Washington, DC   20006
(202) 969-8890 • fax: (202) 969-5612
E-mail: info@CFInst.org
Web site: www.cfinst.org

The nonpartisan, nonprofit CFI combines research and education, task forces, and policy recommendations in an attempt to create change in U.S. campaign finance. The institute focuses on the influence of interest groups in both presidential and congressional elections and the laws that govern them. Comprehensive analysis can be read on the CFI Web site. The CFI has also published such books as *Election After Reform: Money, Politics and the Bipartisan Campaign Reform Act* and *Life After Reform: When the Bipartisan Campaign Reform Act Meets Politics.*

Cato Institute

1000 Massachusetts Ave. NW, Washington, DC   20001-5403
(202) 842-0200 • fax: (202) 842-3490
Web site: www.cato.org

The Cato Institute is a Libertarian think tank that promotes ideals such as limited government, free markets, individual liberty, and peace. The organization contends that campaign finance should be less restricted to ensure fair and competitive elections. Publications such as "Uncompetitive Elections and the American Political System" and "Chapter 9: Campaign Finance" from the *Cato Handbook for Policymakers, 7th Edition*, detail Cato's stance on the issue. In addition to these focused campaign finance works, the institute also regularly publishes the *Cato Journal, Cato's Letter*, and the *Cato Policy Report*.

Center for Governmental Studies (CGS)

10951 W. Pico Blvd., Suite 120, Los Angeles, CA   90064-2184

(310) 470-6590 • fax: (310) 475-3752
E-mail: center@cgs.org
Web site: www.cgs.org

Founded in 1983, CGS helps citizens to become more involved in shaping their communities and their state and local governments through its educational and analytical measures. The center has sought to increase campaign finance transparency through the Campaign Disclosure Project, improve campaign finance reform by drafting laws for both state and local governments, and analyze the effectiveness of public financing in U.S. elections. Reports and commentary on all of these topics can be read on the CGS Web site.

Center for Responsive Politics (CRP)
1101 14th Street NW, Suite 1030
Washington, DC   20005-5635
(202) 857-0044 • fax: (202) 857-7809
E-mail: info@crp.org
Web site: www.opensecrets.org

CRP tracks the influence of money in political elections and reports on it. The center seeks to create a more informed public with regard to the impact of money on elections and to empower citizens to take a more active role in the construction of government. Additionally, CRP advocates for increased governmental transparency and responsiveness. CRP's Web site, OpenSecrets.org provides detailed information about the impact of money in all facets of elections and government. Current reports and analyses provide information about the ongoing issue of campaign finance and contributions.

Federal Election Commission (FEC)
999 E Street NW, Washington, DC   20463
(800) 424-9530
www.fec.gov

The FEC was created in 1975 to be a federal, independent regulatory agency charged with enforcing the laws governing the financing of federal elections. As such, the commission discloses campaign finance information, ensures that candidates comply with the limits and prohibitions on campaign contributions, and supervises the public funding of presidential elections. The president appoints the six commissioners who head the FEC. The FEC Web site provides answers to general questions about campaign finance as well as reports detailing candidates' expenditures and the current law.

Heritage Foundation
214 Massachusetts Ave. NE, Washington, DC 20002-4999
(202) 546-4400 • fax: (202) 546-8328
E-mail: info@heritage.org
Web site: www.heritage.org

The Heritage Foundation advocates for government policies that encourage traditionally conservative values such as free enterprise, competition, and individual responsibility amid limited government and a strong national defense. Writings on campaign finance reform over the past three decades can be found on the organization's Web site. Titles include "Memo to the New Congressional Leadership: How to Improve Proposals for Congressional Earmark and Lobbying Reform," "Campaign Finance Reform: Broad, Vague, and Unenforceable," and "Top Ten Myths About Campaign Finance Reform."

Hoover Institution
434 Galvez Mall, Stanford University
Stanford, CA 94305-6010
(650) 723-1754
Web site: www.hoover.org

The Hoover Institution at Stanford University has sought since its founding in 1959 to preserve the principles of individual, economic, and political freedom; private enterprise; and a representative but limited government. The institution has addressed the issue of campaign finance reform in its publication the *Hoover Digest* and on the Web site Campaign FinanceSite.org. The site provides a historical overview of the issue of campaign finance, as well as current legislation governing money in elections. The Hoover Press published the report *Political Money: Deregulating American Politics: Selected Writings on Campaign Finance Reform.*

Joyce Foundation

70 W. Madison Street, Suite 2750, Chicago, IL   60602
(312) 782-2464 • fax: (312) 782-4160
E-mail: info@joycefdn.org
Web site: www.joycefdn.org

Based in the Great Lakes region of the United States, the Joyce Foundation works to preserve the natural environment of this area as well as the well-being and livelihood of its inhabitants. The foundation believes that one important method of achieving these goals is to advance campaign finance reform, which will ensure that the voices of ordinary citizens and the groups representing their views are reflected in policy-making decisions. Reports and newsletters detailing the organization's views on current efforts to reform campaign finance can be read on the Joyce Foundation Web site.

National Institute on Money in State Politics

833 N. Last Chance Gulch, 2nd Floor, Helena, MT   59601
(406) 449-2480 • fax: (406) 457-2091
Web site: www.followthemoney.org

The National Institute on Money in State Politics is a nonpartisan, nonprofit organization dedicated to providing detailed information about the impact of campaign contributions on state-level elections and policy-making. The institute hopes to increase governmental transparency at the state level by informing the citizenry through its comprehensive Web site. Visitors to the site can find information about campaign finance in their district as well as information about national contributions and lobbying efforts. The Web site also provides detailed reports such as "Greasing the Wheels: The Crossroads of Campaign Money & Transportation Policy," "Money Fuels Power Measures," and "Building Their Immunity."

Public Campaign

1320 19th Street NW, Suite M-1, Washington, DC   20036
(202) 293-0222 • fax: (202) 293-0202
E-mail: info@publicampaign.org
Web site: www.publicampaign.org

Public Campaign is working to enact sweeping political finance reform that will reduce the influence of big, special-interest-group money in American elections and provide a voice for individuals who currently lack representation in the campaign finance system. The organization's Web site provides up-to-date information about campaign finance and the lacking representation of minority groups. The campaign also contributes to the Color of Money Project, whose Web site, *ColorofMoney.org*, breaks down campaign contributions by race, ethnicity, and neighborhood.

Bibliography

Books

Bruce Ackerman and Ian Ayres
Voting with Dollars: A New Paradigm for Campaign Finance. New Haven, CT: Yale University Press, 2004.

Anthony Corrado, Thomas E. Mann, and Trevor Potter, eds.
Inside the Campaign Finance Battle: Court Testimony on the New Reforms. Washington, DC: Brookings Institution Press, 2003.

Anthony Corrado et al.
The New Campaign Finance Sourcebook. Washington, DC: Brookings Institution Press, 2005.

David Donnelly, Janice Fine, and Ellen S. Miller
Are Elections for Sale? Boston, MA: Beacon Press, 2001.

Michael M. Franz
Choices and Changes: Interest Groups in the Electoral Process. Philadelphia: Temple University Press, 2008.

Michael M. Franz et al.
Campaign Advertising and American Democracy. Philadelphia: Temple University Press, 2007.

Kurt Hohenstein
Coining Corruption: The Making of the American Campaign Finance System. DeKalb, IL: Northern Illinois University Press, 2007.

Raymond J.
La Raja

Small Change: Money, Political Parties, and Campaign Finance Reform. Ann Arbor, MI: University of Michigan Press, 2008.

Costas
Panagopoulos

Politicking Online: The Transformation of Election Campaign Communications. Piscataway, NJ: Rutgers University Press, 2009.

Joshua
Rosenkranz

Buckley Stops Here: Loosening the Judicial Stranglehold on Campaign Finance. New York, NY: Century Foundation Press, 1998.

John Samples

The Fallacy of Campaign Finance Reform. Chicago, IL: University of Chicago Press, 2006.

Jerrold E.
Schneider

Campaign Finance Reform and the Future of the Democratic Party. New York, NY: Routledge, 2002.

David A. Schultz

Money, Politics, and Campaign Finance Reform Law in the States. Durham, NC: Carolina Academic Press, 2002.

Bradley A. Smith

Unfree Speech: The Folly of Campaign Finance Reform. Princeton, NJ: Princeton University Press, 2001.

Rodney A. Smith

Money, Power, & Elections: How Campaign Finance Reform Subverts American Democracy. Baton Rouge: Louisiana State University Press, 2006.

Melvin I. Urofsky   *Money and Free Speech: Campaign Finance Reform and the Courts.* Lawrence, KS: University Press of Kansas, 2005.

Peter J. Wallison   *Better Parties, Better Government: A Realistic Program for Campaign Finance Reform.* Washington, DC: AEI Press, 2009.

Periodicals

Ari Berman   "Making Elections Fair," *Nation*, April 30, 2007.

Emily Cadei   "Stretching the Reach of Soft Money," *CQ Weekly*, May 5, 2008.

John Cochran   "Campaign Finance's Deregulation Option," *CQ Weekly*, July 9, 2007.

David Corn   "Play Dirty for Me," *Mother Jones*, March/April 2008.

Ann Coulter   "How to Keep Reagan out of Office," *Human Events*, February 25, 2008.

Tom De Luca   "Free Speech, Political Equality, and Campaign Finance Reform: A Paradox for Democracy?" *New Political Science*, June 2007.

Economist   "Free Speech for Me, but Not for Thee," September 12, 2009.

Steve Forbes   "Those Corrosive Money Laws—Junk 'Em," *Forbes*, December 8, 2008.

Robert H. Frank "Untying a Knot in Campaign Finance," *New York Times*, July 6, 2008.

Michael Humphrey "Reforming an 'Untenable' System," *National Catholic Reporter*, October 3, 2008.

Jeremy P. Jacobs "The Case That Could Change the Race," *Politics*, October 2009.

Sara Jerome "Campaign Finance Law Under Siege," *National Journal*, November 21, 2009.

Matt Kelley and Fredreka Schouten "Wealthy Few Provide Much of the Cash for Independent Political Groups," *USA Today*, July 22, 2008.

Danielle Knight "A Bunch of Money Trouble," *U.S. News & World Report*, October 1, 2007.

Nathan Koppel "Corruption Cases Renew Debate on Campaign-Finance Laws," *Wall Street Journal*, January 15, 2009.

John R. Lott, Jr. and Bradley A. Smith "Campaign-Finance Breakdown," *Wall Street Journal*, March 5, 2008.

Michael Luo "The Myth of the Small Donor," *New York Times*, November 25, 2008.

Warren Richey "Supreme Court: Campaign Finance Overhaul in 'Hillary' Case?" *Christian Science Monitor*, September 8, 2009.

Karl Rove	"McCain Couldn't Compete with Obama's Money," *Wall Street Journal*, December 4, 2008.
Stuart Taylor, Jr.	"Polarizing Campaign Finance Law," *National Journal*, June 30, 2007.
Bara Vaida	"A Comeback for Issue Ads?" *National Journal*, September 8, 2007.
David Weigel	"More Money, No Problem," *Reason*, May 2007.

Index